# INDIAN Birds

To a great fraternity —
the Indian Army

BRIJBASI



Published by Brijbasi Printers Pvt. Ltd.
E-46/11, Okhla Industrial Area, Phase II,
New Delhi-110 020



Published 1994

Designed by GOPI GAJWANI

Phototypeset by Alphabets, New Delhi

Printed and bound in Singapore

ISBN 81-7107-031-0

INDIAN
Birds
by R.K. Gaur

# FOREWORD

With our vast and varied terrain conditions, encompassing virtually every type of geographical feature, we are home to a large number of birds and also play host to several more varieties, who are winter visitors. Unfortunately, for one reason or another most of us do not have access to the requisite source material and specialised information that is so vitally important if we are to enjoy our flora and fauna more intimately, and to develop the empathy which will result in an increased concern for their well-being. This little book seeks to bridge that gap.

This story starts a few years ago, when I was commanding a Division in Ladakh and Ram Gaur joined me as my deputy. Though we were together in the Academy, our paths never crossed in the interim, but stories kept drifting back about this professional oddity, who seemed to spend a lot of time on his environment and had developed, over the years an increasing passion for it. During our first interview I asked him what he would like to do, since there was not enough work for both of us. With a straight face he told me that he would gladly let me work without interference, while he would concentrate on documenting the life in Ladakh. I accepted this broad division of duty, but only after emphasising that he was my deputy and not vice versa. The next two years passed happily enough.

He was mainly instrumental in changing the general perception of the Army-man from that of a poacher to a conservationist and has, over the years, enhanced his reputation and spread the message of conservation in a number of different forums, to increasingly appreciative audiences. Our initial venture was a pilot project for the protection of the Black Necked Crane and from those beginnings has developed the Army's credo.

I do hope that this beautifully produced book will enable more of our people to share his dreams. A deep and abiding interest in nature and the ability to live in harmony with our environment are mutually supporting endeavours, for which we can never do enough if we are to continue to share nature's bounty.

I congratulate Ram Gaur and his publisher for this delightful venture. I am confident that it will be very well received.

19 June, 1993

(SF RODRIGUES)
*General*

# Introduction

In my early Army days, I often heard the old tenet that a soldier isn't 'complete' if he does not hunt. Military training the world over recognizes the instinct to kill as the soldier's most basic quality, and when he is not killing on the battlefield, what better target than wild animals and birds to keep the instinct alive? There is no doubt that hunting puts to test all the skills a soldier needs to keep himself in fighting trim. In order to track his quarry down, he must know the terrain and be familiar with the art of reconnaissance; he must know the habits and movements of the prey, which involves keen observation and surveillance; and only the most effective fieldcraft comprising camouflage and stalking will help him get within striking range. The final act of killing not only perfects his ability to kill, it also prepares him psychologically for that moment when he may actually have to kill another human being in war.

Belonging to an orthodox, vegetarian family I had no interest in hunting. I therefore had a handicap in convincing my peers and my seniors that I could be accepted in the fraternity. Since, however, I was a very good shot on the range, my Commanding Officer cleverly challenged me to prove my skill against live, elusive targets. And so I became his close companion on frequent hunting trips in Saurashtra and in Kashmir. I must confess that the thrill of locating, stalking, and bringing down an animal or a bird is heady. But one day a senior pointed out that it was unethical for me to kill if I did not eat meat. Since then I have confined my shooting of birds and animals to the camera. I might add that its thrill, and its relevance to soldiering, match any pursuits with the gun.

In my youth, conservation talk had not yet made the cocktail circuit and things such as birdwatching were equated with star-gazing and considered equally inane and unsoldierly. I am neither a professional cameraman nor an ornithologist. My only excuse for intruding into this field was my keen interest in nature, for which I could not have chosen a better combination of profession and leisure pursuit. The Army offers an ideal opportunity for developing a close affinity with nature, taking you where others cannot or will not go, where being in harmony with the environment adds to your professional competence and where you actually begin to see at close range the intricate web of the ecological balance. I am lucky to have belonged to this great fraternity—the Indian Army—and have availed myself of every opportunity it offered.

I have found great fulfilment in documenting all aspects of life — seasons, flowers and other plant life, insects, birds, animals and people and their habits and activities. I have had even more pleasure sharing my experience with the family and with friends, through slide presentations, transporting them to distant places they could not have visited; reliving myself all those wonderful moments over and over again. The pictures presented in this portfolio have been selected out of many decades of shutterbugging. I would feel very encouraged if this effort inspires others to appreciate the beauty of Indian birds, realize their significance in the scheme of nature and develop an abiding concern to preserve this valuable national heritage.

I wish to acknowledge my gratitude to Gen S F Rodrigues, PVSM, VSM, ADC, the Chief of Army Staff, who was my GOC in Ladakh, and Padma Bhushan Lt Gen M L Chibber, PVSM, AVSM, erstwhile GOC-in-C, Northern Command who ignored my escapades and encouraged and assisted me to continue my interest in photography. Thanks are due also to my colleagues Maj Gen A K Verma, AVSM and Lt Gen M L Dar, AVSM and my friend Tsering Nurbu, all extremely keen and competent wildlifers, who patiently initiated me into the lore. Two very senior foresters, Mir Inayatullah, erstwhile Chief Wildlife Warden of Jammu and Kashmir, and Shri V D Sharma, Chief Wildlife Warden, Rajasthan, provided me every facility in their respective states, for which I wish to thank them. I am grateful to Rajesh Bedi for his esteemed advice at every stage of this book, to Sharad Gaur for invaluable technical assistance in this compilation, to my family for putting up with the infernal nuisance of such an activity, and to my bosses for being indulgent with my unsoldierly pursuits.

R.K. Gaur

# India: The Bird Haven

In more ways than one, India is a unique land, for in no other single country or area of comparable size can you find such extremes of physical conditions and natural diversity. From the nearly rainless desert to the rainiest place on earth, from hot salt flats to snow-clad peaks, with a vast area of ocean shores, mangroves, great river systems and their plains, and large lakes and daunting mountain ranges, India has nearly every type of climate and terrain.

India's biological diversity is also unparalleled. On a land area of just 2 per cent of the Earth's surface, it supports over 5 per cent of the world's life forms. The country's wildlife comprises over 75,000 animal species which include 300 species of mammals, and 1,200 of birds. In addition there are over 15,000 species of flowering plants.

This diversity is most beautifully exemplified by Indian birds. About 8,650 bird species, representing 27 living Orders and 155 Families, have been described in the world so far. Of this total, India has over 1,200 species from 20 Orders and 17 Families. That makes it one sixth of the world's total avian diversity on a land mass only one fiftieth of the earth!

India lies at the trijunction of three important biogeographic provinces of the earth—Ethiopian (African), Palaearctic (European and North Asian), and Oriental (of which it forms a part along with South East Asia). As a result its bird life has elements from all the three, besides many forms which are uniquely Indian. The characteristic bird families of this region include pheasants, leafbirds, pittas, and flowerpeckers. Some bird families which occur throughout the tropics include pelicans, ibises, trogons, barbets, parrots, and cuckoos. Birds of prey, owls, crows, and shorebirds have a worldwide distribution. Many of India's most characteristic birds are in families which occur only in the Old World tropics. These include hornbills, sunbirds, bulbuls, babblers, and cuckoo-shrikes, while the leafbirds or fruitsuckers are confined to the Oriental region. Some families are particularly richly represented in India. These include forest species such as woodpeckers, pigeons, owls, cuckoos, pheasants, drongos, crows, minivets, babblers, flycatchers, and warblers.

Since India presents within itself such a variety of habitats and physiographic conditions, it has been further sub-divided into faunal sub regions to facilitate the study of the distribution of animal life in the region. Several classifications are currently in use, some of which identify as many as 10 main biogeographic zones in India, with 25 provinces or sub-zones. However, for the limited purpose of understanding the gross distribution of birds on the Indian mainland, the following simple classification should suffice.

### The Himalayan Mountain System Sub-Region

The major factor influencing the distribution of life in this region is altitude. A 100 metre rise in altitude is equivalent to a 10° increase in latitude. Thus, elevations of 3,500 metres and above in the Himalaya have near-Arctic conditions. There are also distinct East-West variations, resulting from a gradual decline in monsoon rainfall as one moves westward. The Himalayan zone has various sub-systems. These comprise the foothills (including the Shivalik ranges with their *bhabhar* and *terai* formations), the Western Himalaya, and the Eastern Himalaya.

The *bhabhar* in the lower Himalaya and in the foothills is a tract characterized by deep boulder deposits. The habitat is relatively dry because of the low water table and extremely high percolation and run-off. In sharp contrast, the *terai*, once an unbroken belt of forest and swampy grassland habitats, consists of huge deposits of alluvial silt brought down by the mountain streams. The water table is high, and the drainage poor, resulting in high humidity conditions. Because of its fertile soils and forest wealth, the *terai* has become one of the worst ravaged wildlife habitats in the country — extensively colonized by agriculturists, logged for timber, and clearfelled for habitation. Nevertheless, it remains one of the richest areas of bird diversity in India, with sanctuaries such as Dudhwa recording nearly 470 bird species. The notable bird groups of this region include red junglefowl, kalij and chir pheasants, floricans, woodpeckers, swamp partridges, forest eagles and owls, orioles, pittas, minivets, bulbuls, and migratory waterfowl. The pink-headed duck was once quite common in the eastern part of the *terai*, seen as far south as Bihar. But it has not been observed since 1935 and is feared to be extinct.

South of the eastern end of the Indian *terai* lies a unique mangrove ecosystem, the Sunderban, which India shares with Bangladesh. Of the 8,000-odd square kilometre mangrove area, nearly 2,500 square kilometres lie within India. It is a maze of mangroves and coastal forests interspersed with tidal creeks, into which the deltas of the Ganga and the Brahmaputra drain. The habitat is an amazing mix of high salinity as well as freshwater areas and is subject to periodic tidal inundation. Among the characteristic birds of this habitat are large egrets, white stork, adjutant stork, fishing eagles, ospreys, and several species of ducks and geese.

The Western Himalaya is a high-altitude region extending from Ladakh to Kumaon, with habitats ranging from pine forests in the 1,500-2,500 metre belt; rhododendron, birch, and dwarf hill bamboo forests mixed with alpine pastures extending from these altitudes up to the snow line; and the arctic zone extending above 3,500 metres. In the arctic zone lies the high-altitude cold desert plateau of Ladakh, which forms the extreme North West frontier of the country. Barheaded geese, brahminy ducks, redshanks, wheatears, accentors, and Mongolian plovers are some of the birds whose breeding ranges have their southern limits in Ladakh. The only blacknecked cranes in India are found here. Ladakh also happens to form a very important transit route for several of the migrants coming into India over the high mountain passes. The Western Himalaya is particularly rich in the high-altitude gallinaceous species including snowcocks, partridges, and pheasants. A bewildering variety of vultures, kites, eagles, falcons, finches, larks, buntings, sparrows, pipits, bulbuls, wagtails, chats, tits, warblers, choughs, ravens, and magpies are also found here.

The Eastern Himalaya is a zone characterized by high rainfall and relatively lower snowfall as compared to the Western Himalaya. Foothills in this region are called *duars*. The habitats of this zone include wet and moist evergreen forests, with an abundance of orchids, mosses, and lichens.

The Indo-Chinese and Indo-Malayan elements of India's bird life become well marked as one moves eastward through this zone. Starting from a typical Himalayan avian diversity, the Eastern Himalaya exhibits a gradual transition, as bird species with Malayan affinities become predominant, in some cases replacing their Indian counterparts. Hornbills, malkohas, pheasants, scarlet minivets, tits, whitewinged wood ducks, hill mynas, etc. are the better known species of this zone.

### The Indian Peninsular Sub-Region

The Indian Peninsula occupies the larger part of the mainland, extending right up to the southern tip. Two broad zones are identifiable in this region—the tropical deciduous woodlands and the desert.

The Tropical Deciduous Woodlands sub-zone includes a vast area of deciduous forests and their extensions into the drainage basin of the Ganga river system. The forest habitats include moist to dry scrub thorn types, with some areas of grasslands. A few ancient mountain ranges, including the Aravali, the Vindhya, the Satpura, and the Similipal, dot this zone. The wetlands, scrub forests, and grasslands of this zone form very important bird habitats. Among the hundreds of bird species found over this region, the most notable are floricans, bustards, partridges, peafowl, junglefowl, ducks and geese, and several waders, besides ibises, herons, cormorants, and pelicans.

The Thar, or Indian Desert, is the area lying to the west of the Aravali range and just east of the Indus valley. Ecologically, this zone would also include the salt flats of the Rann of Kachchh, lying South-West of the Thar. The Desert is a zone of extreme aridity, scanty rainfall, high winds and sand storms, hot days and low night temperatures.

Among the important bird families of the Thar are the common and the painted sandgrouse, partridges, bustards, an extremely rich array of raptors (including eagles, buzzards, harriers, hawks, kites, and falcons), vultures, demoiselle cranes found seasonally on the wetlands, flamingos in the Little Rann, and hordes of desert country and thorn scrub birds, including larks, warblers, pipits, munias, sparrows etcetera.

### The Tropical Evergreen, or the Indo-Malayan Sub-Region

This sub-region consists of medium to heavy rainfall areas, with wet or moist evergreen and semi-evergreen forests. It includes North Eastern India and the Western Ghats region in the South, including the Malabar Coast.

The major bird families notable in this zone are trogons, hornbills, woodpeckers, nuthatches, junglefowl, paradise flycatchers, forest eagles and owls, nightjars, partridges, quails, hill mynas etcetera.

## FOR THE BIRDER

What exactly is it about birds that attracts us? Birds are different things to different people. The uninterested casual onlooker finds them nothing more than noisy flying creatures that occasionally dirty his dress. The serious naturalist sees them not just as subjects of lifelong study and a source of pleasure, but as indicators of environmental health and, indeed, of the quality of our own life.

This section is meant primarily as a guide for the amateur birder, providing brief tips on the various marvellous facets of bird life that one can observe without going to any great length and without requiring too much equipment.

### The Life of Birds

Birds are all around us, from right inside our homes to the most bleak and inhospitable snow-bound peaks and scorching deserts. In fact, you can see birds in habitats where even mammals, despite all their ingenuity and evolutionary superiority, cannot survive. In this sense, birds are the only truly ubiquitous large animals.

### Flight

With the exception of the bats, birds are the only truly flying vertebrates. They are also the fastest of animals. The spine- tailed swift has been recorded flying at 170 kilometres an hour. Falcons can dive in the air at more than 125 kilometres an hour. There are, of course, birds that cannot fly! But even among these, an ostrich can outrun a horse and some penguins can paddle through ice-cold water at speeds of over 40 kilometres per hour.

Since flying needs vast amounts of energy, birds have devised means of energy conservation in every aspect of their life, inclusive of flying. Several birds glide or soar in the air. They do so by making use of such natural air phenomena as thermals, breezes, tidal winds, etc. Vultures and eagles can be seen soaring for hours without flapping their wings. Albatrosses are perhaps the ultimate in this category. They wander over ocean waves for months at a stretch, using the energy of the air currents produced by the sea's wave action. In fact, their own flight power is so limited that most of the species have not been able to cross the belt of the calm seas at the Equator and they are found in the southern hemisphere only. There are birds, on the other hand, whose flight is so developed that not only can they hover at the same spot in the air but even fly backwards! Hummingbirds and sunbirds do this to position themselves precisely in front of flowers, so that they can use their long beaks to get at the nectar. Kestrels can also hover in the air to scan the ground beneath for prey, but they do this by flying against the breeze and by adjusting their flapping to balance the forward and backward motions.

The structure that makes bird flight possible, and is found in no other animal, is of course the feather. Feathers not only help a bird fly, they also give it colour, shape, warmth and, in many cases, camouflage. Most birds have mechanisms such as interlocking feather barbs and oil glands that make feathers water-repellent, strong and supple, and they spend long periods, preening and grooming to retain flying fitness. Though extremely light, feathers constitute nearly 15%

of the bird's weight. You can judge this from the following examples. A mallard duck has 12,000 feathers; the swan has 25,000, whilst even the small house sparrow has nearly 3,500 feathers in winter and 500 less in summer.

### Plumage and Feathers

Many birds change colour during the year. The tips of the feathers seasonally wear away, revealing the basal parts which may be a different colour. Most birds shed their feathers at least once a year to grow new ones. This process of moulting may happen in phases, so the bird goes through several stages of changing colours, or all at one go, in which case the bird remains shaggy and flightless until the new plumage is developed. The most spectacular changes in plumage are seen just before the onset of the breeding season, especially in those species which depend on courtship displays for the selection of their mates and the reproduction of their race. It is usually the male bird which is more colourful, which helps to attract the females but repels rival males. But amongst the polyandrous birds, the female is more attractive and more active in pursuing the male bird. Such birds leave the care and feeding of the young to the male, which is considered to be a higher evolutionary stage!

### Designs for Survival

The bird body is a marvel of nature's engineering. Everything in it is built for speed and for a hectic pace of life. Bird metabolism is the highest in the animal kingdom. Their body temperatures remain constant at a few degrees above the mammalian body temperatures (between 39 and 44 degrees Celsius, depending on the species) regardless of the temperature outside. As an adaptation, a few birds such as swifts and hummingbirds have even evolved the ability to undergo a temporary drop in body temperature to tide over extremely cold periods. But for most birds, this constancy of temperature provides them with an edge over others, enabling them to occupy even those niches where others cannot survive—for example, extremely hot deserts or high-altitude arctic environments and the polar ice caps.

The bones in a bird's skeleton are hollow (with struts) and extremely light, yet quite strong. This helps to reduce the total body weight, which facilitates flying. In a pelican weighing 25 lbs, the total weight of the skeleton is no more than 1.5 lbs. There are other adaptations, too. The bird body is streamlined so as to offer minimal wind resistance during flight. The keel is enlarged and to it are anchored the flight muscles—the specialized and modified breast muscles—that pack the amazing power in a bird's flight. To aid flight further, the body has several air sacs which can be variably inflated to provide buoyancy. The hollow bones are connected to air sacs and due to a unique breathing mechanism, oxygen is supplied to the lungs from this source during exhalation. The aerodynamics of the bird wing is also an amazing field of study. As a matter of fact, from the days of the mythological Daedalus, who tried flying with the aid of artificial wings, to modern streamlined aircraft designs, the flight of birds has been the source of both inspiration and knowledge for aeronautical engineering.

### Activity

Birds are almost always doing something or the other. Even when they are visibly not active, they are not exactly 'asleep' because they are alert at all times and watchful of their surroundings. Therefore, the bulk of a birdwatcher's work relates to observing the activities of birds and trying to find out what they are doing, and how frequently, how they do it, why they do it, and so on. The other aspect of observation relates to the surroundings in which birds live, in particular how they interact with it in trying to feed, breed, and survive and how the environment affects them. The list of activities and happenings in a bird's life is endless and trying to describe each thing will be beyond the scope of this book. Nevertheless, small notes on some of the more noteworthy aspects of bird life follow, in the hope that the beginner, for whom this section is primarily intended, will find some useful tips for planning his field activities and arranging his priorities.

### Habitats

Although birds are rather omnipresent creatures, not every bird occurs just anywhere. It is interesting to observe how different species, or families, of birds prefer to spend their time in different places possessing those special conditions that suit them the most. Such places are termed habitats. Within these habitats are many different micro-addresses called niches which denote a bird's place in terms of space, time, and activity. It is not just coincidence that you repeatedly find woodpeckers on tree trunks with cracked bark,and waders only on the shallows. Even in a given habitat, the species found there operate within their allocated range of niches, thus averting competition over time and space. On the same tree you may find over a dozen species of birds at the same time, but all using different portions of the tree for their activities. Yet some other species will be visiting the same tree at different times of the day or night, for different purposes. A careful birdwatcher soon begins to perceive these significant pointers which assist in location and identification of birds.

### Feeding

To fuel their high rate of metabolism, birds must spend a large part of their time feeding, or gathering food. This becomes all the more evident when they have young in the nest, are preparing for their next breeding cycle, or for a migratory journey.

The observation of feeding in birds takes into account such things as the structure and adaptation of their beaks and feet, since these are intricately linked with each bird's habitat and food choice. Incidentally birds do not have teeth. The beaks themselves are modified, elongated hardened lips. Grain-eating birds use their strong beaks and palate bones, which enable them to crack open nuts, and to grind grain and seeds. Many of them eat grit to further facilitate the grinding action in the gizzards. Most of the fruit-eating species subsist on the pulp but ingest the seeds in their diet, to excrete them elsewhere. Since the seeds retain their germinating power, and are covered with rich nutrients in the excreta, such birds become important agents in the dispersal of the food plants. Nectar feeders subsist wholly or partly on the nectar of flowers, for which their beaks are thin and long and have special adaptations like tubular tongues for sucking by piston action. Raptors have hooked, sharp, strong beaks for tearing flesh. Spatulate beaks with special strainer-like structures clearly indicate the filter feeding nature of certain birds like flamingos; while oystercatchers, as the name suggests, can pry open or break the shells of their molluscan prey, using their bills as lever.

Bird feet are specially adapted for survival in the specific habitat of each species, and in many cases aid the bird in such activities as hunting, holding, manipulating, tearing, clinging, etc. Ducks and geese have webbed feet that serve as swimming paddles; jacanas and coots live and breed amidst floating weeds and broad-leaved aquatic plants,like lilies, for which their toes are extremely long to afford them better purchase on a floating and bobbing substratum; storks, flamingos, and several other wading birds have elongated legs to facilitate foraging in shallow water and mud; birds of prey such as eagles, hawks, falcons, and owls, and carrion eaters like vultures have strong, hooked talons in their toes, for gripping and tearing flesh. Perching birds have a special muscular mechanism that is activated by the bird's own weight and locks their toes tightly around the perch, so that the bird will not fall even when it is sleeping. A most fascinating adaptation—the spur—is seen in the legs of the cock in a few gallinaceous birds such as junglefowl and spurfowl. These birds are pugnaciously territorial and rival males actually use the spurred legs in vicious kicking fights, often injuring each other.

The menu of carnivorous birds is infinitely diverse. Depending on their individual sizes, beak adaptations and habitat, these species prey on small mammals, other birds, amphibians, reptiles, fishes, insects, spiders, worms, molluscs, etc. A few eat carcasses.

While watching a group of social feeders one can discover various forms of behaviour and interaction among the members of the flock. These include hierarchy, kinship, threats and aggressive postures, and mutual feeding. Several other interesting facets of bird feeding can also be studied, such as the impact on local populations of their prey species, their role in the control of certain pest populations, seasonality in the choice of food, the impact of some species on crops or plantations, their role as pollinators of certain plant species, etcetera.

### Migration

Each winter, when habitats in North and Central Asia and in some parts of Europe become inhospitable due to the advancing cold and the disappearance of food under the snow cover, large numbers of birds that breed in these areas in the summer undertake migratory journeys mainly along major river routes to spend the winter in more hospitable quarters. That is the reason why large flocks of starlings, several species of waterfowl, some species of wagtails, and many other birds, which are not seen for the rest of the year, suddenly appear towards the end of autumn, staying on with us till the end of winter. There are also local migrants, birds that breed and reside exclusively within India but journey between their breeding and wintering areas seasonally. Pittas, orioles, many waders, some wagtails, brahminy ducks and barheaded geese, and several other species are good examples of such migration. In addition, there are temporary phenomena which trigger sudden influx of birds from surrounding areas, or a sudden exodus. The emergence of the winged phase of termites in a forest invites hordes of bee-eaters, flycatchers and the like. Trees in bloom or with seasonal fruit become centres of concentration for fruit-eating and nectar-sucking birds, like parakeets, sunbirds and flower peckers. Similarly, prolonged adversities in habitat conditions may force some resident species to move away temporarily to more congenial areas. In some regions this occurs fairly regularly because of the seasonal nature of such disturbances and is then akin to regular migration. This is also nature's protective mechanism to allow regeneration of the food resource and to prevent over-exploitation.

Precise and detailed information about the phenomenon of migration to and from India is very scanty and there is much scope for gathering data and researching this extremely interesting aspect of bird life. Depending on the degree to which one wants to delve, one could 'graduate' from simple birdwatching to participating in censuses of migratory waterfowl or in bird-ringing experiments.

### Reproduction

Every year, birds set about courtship, pairing, laying eggs and raising the young, to ensure the continuance of their species. Amongst some species there are bachelor birds who help in feeding and guarding the young of their kin, instead of breeding their own. If a clutch is destroyed, many species lay again. The study of breeding in birds is a very important field of study. It is even more so in India, because we still do not know very much about most of our breeding species. The various facets of bird breeding which provide scope for field observation and documentation include courtship behaviour and displays; bird nests and nesting behaviour; eggs, their sizes and colours, incubation behaviour; division of labour between the sexes during nest building, incubation and chick rearing; incubation periods and their local or seasonal variations; feeding and cleaning of the young; and fledging periods.

In general, breeding seasons in sub-tropical India are not so well defined as in the colder parts, which are akin to temperate and arctic areas. While individual species and related families do have their clear-cut seasons, these are influenced by geographical position and local climate. Breeding periods tend to be more concentrated and brief in the colder climes and more diffuse in the warmer plains and the peninsula. Three overlapping breeding seasons can be identified in India. Wherever in the plains there is a clear-cut winter, the advent of spring, around March, brings to a peak the breeding activity of several of our common species. In the colder, higher altitudes, this begins only around June/July because that is when spring-like conditions prevail. Over most of equatorial and sub-equatorial India, one major breeding season follows the advance of the South West monsoon. Most aquatic birds, herons, storks, and some insectivorous species breed in this season, so as to synchronise the arrival of their young with the maximum availability of aquatic food and insects. Similarly, the bigger birds of prey and the owls breed in a diffuse period from October to March, when the young of the monsoon breeding birds have left the protection of their nests and many of the winter migrants have arrived. This ensures that their own young — prolific eaters — will have no dearth of food. Birds which nest on or close to the ground, as also those which build their nests by or on the water bodies affected by the monsoon, must finish rearing their babies before their nesting sites are disturbed by the rains. These species breed a month or two ahead of the monsoon's arrival in their region. For obvious reasons, the chicks of ground-nesting birds are precocial.

Courtship behaviour among Indian birds is extremely diverse. From the absolutely monogamous and pair-bonded sarus cranes to the polygamous weaver birds or polyandrous jacanas, and from the simple songs of some passerines to the elaborate nuptial displays of floricans and cranes and spectacular aerobatics of some raptors there is a whole range of interesting behaviour patterns that can be observed.

Nests and nesting behaviour also provide an equally absorbing variety for study. Nesting patterns range from those of the simpleton lapwing, who lays in a bare scrape in the ground, to some of the most elaborate nesters seen anywhere. In the latter category one could mention the intricately woven grass and twig nest of the weaver bird, or the deftly stitched purse nest of the tailor bird. Nesting and egg-laying habits are equally diverse. The parasitic cuckoos just don't take the trouble of building a nest; instead, they fool the incubating parents of other species to foster their eggs, smuggled into the clutch of the latter. Hornbill fathers are known for sealing or 'walling in' the incubating mother inside the nest hole, while they themselves take on the duties of guarding the nest and bringing food for the family, handing it in through a narrow slit in the mud wall of the nest. Then there are some species of babblers which have discovered the economy and security of communal nesting. Therefore several females lay their eggs in a common nest and jointly share the brooding and rearing responsibilities. The larger raptors keep to the same territory over the years and re-use the same nest year after year, making repairs and modifications as the need arises.

Bird parents employ a wide variety of techniques for protection of the young. Some defenceless birds like doves and bulbuls make their nests close to drongo nests because drongos are pugnacious fighters, keeping at bay much larger raptors. The nests are carefully camouflaged, female birds and dependent chicks are dull and cryptically coloured. At least one parent is always present in or near the nest while the other is foraging. Threat posture, violent protest, alarm calls and fierce attacks, sometimes collective mobbing or distraction display, are used to drive away or divert a predator. They take great care when bringing food for the young. The approach to the nest is seldom direct. The parents usually land some distance away from the nest and after ensuring that no predator is around, they proceed to the young eagerly waiting with mouths agape. Even the droppings of the young are picked up by the parents and disposed of elsewhere, both for hygiene as well as for concealing the location of the nest.

### What's in a Name?

For the majority of new birders the task of remembering the convoluted Latin terminology associated with bird names, and their classification, appears too daunting. It tends to kill all their early enthusiasm. The result is that while many people are becoming interested in the field, only some of them are able to really comprehend the relationships and affinities in the vast kingdom of birds. Yet, bird nomenclature needn't be such a scare. I think this introduction would end best with some simple tips on how to understand, and even more than that, appreciate bird names.

I will not go into the details of the higher levels of classification. That is not the scope of this book. Suffice it to say that within the class Aves there are 27 Orders into which all the living birds have been grouped, depending on their evolutionary relationship. Thus, parrots and related birds — parakeets, lorikeets — come in one Order, while all storks and related birds such as ibises, spoonbills, flamingos, herons, egrets and bitterns form another separate Order. Within each Order, we recognize smaller units, called Families, depending on identifiable sets of similarities that can be used to sub-group the birds. Thus, while storks and relatives are one Order — the Ciconiiformes — the storks are more closely related among themselves than with ibises and spoonbills; and so on. Therefore, we have 4 Families in the Ciconiiformes Order: Ciconiidae consisting of all stroks, Threskiornithidae comprising the ibises and spoonbills, Ardeidae which includes herons, egrets and bitterns, and Phoenicopteridae comprising just the flamingos. To use an analogy, if an Order is a tribe, then the Families are its smaller clans.

Every bird that has been tentatively or definitively identified and assigned to one of the 155 bird Families in the 27 Orders is given a unique name, using the Binomial Nomenclature introduced by Linnaeus. It thus gets a Latin name consisting of two portions — accepted internationally by convention, so as to remove the confusion of local and regional languages and the multiplicity of names used for a single species. The first, its Genus or Generic name (plural Genera), is analogous to our surname or family name; while the second portion, Species, is like a personal or Christian name. The Genus includes all closely related birds conforming to that description, found anywhere. Sometimes, a bird belonging to the same Genus may be given another equivalent Generic name by consensus. But it is the Species which truly refers to a discrete population of birds which are capable of breeding among themselves, and are separated from other Species of the same Genus by biological or behavioural differences so that the two cannot normally interbreed even if they live together. Thus, while all egrets fall under the Genus *Egretta* (or *Bubulcus* of some authors), we have four distinct species in India — little egret, *E. garzetta;* median egret, E. *intermedia;* large egret, *E. alba;* and cattle egret, *Bubulcus ibis.*

Modern taxonomy has added a third level of nomenclature. It now identifies a Sub-species or Geographical Race — an even smaller unit of a Species — identified on the basis of very minute differences brought about by long isolation, or by diverse environmental conditions. But unless you are really interested in making a serious affair of it, you need not go any further than the Genus and the Species, since that is enough to demarcate every 'kind' of bird there is. An understanding of their common English names could also suffice, as even these are descriptive enough to help identify a bird. What is more important is to understand the meanings of these names and enjoy their interpretations. Many of these terms are descriptors of size, colour or some distinctive feature of the bird concerned (e.g. alba, nigra, minor, flava, brunnicephalus). Several describe the region where the bird lives, or was believed to be a native of, when named (e.g. indica, bengalensis, sindensis, ceylonensis). I could have attempted to translate the names of all the 1,200-odd species found in India, but scattered among the picture captions you will find interesting meanings, mythological connections, behavioural similes, and other terms which, besides being pointers to the identities of bird species, are enjoyable to know by themselves, and add a whole new meaning to the way you look at little things around you. With a little bit of practice, you will begin to interpret the names on your own and, who knows, you might someday name a bird or two. If nothing else, your Latin will certainly improve!

# Bird Sanctuaries in India

India has been able to preserve some of her natural splendour in the face of severe pressures from environmentally destructive development activity and a bursting population. Today, most of the country's wildlife finds refuge in a number of National Parks and Sanctuaries, set aside as banks of biological diversity in selected areas. These reserves must serve a dual function—both as repositories of wildlife and as places for enhancing public awareness of the need for conservation.

Because of their ubiquitous nature and extreme adaptability, birds thrive in all protected areas and one could visit just about any of our wildlife reserves to observe their diversity. There are, however, several sanctuaries in India which are known primarily for their bird populations. Some of these were, in fact, set up as Bird Sanctuaries or National Parks. In the section that follows, I have attempted to summarize, for the benefit of the lay reader, some useful information on the better known and more accessible of our bird sanctuaries. This I have done in the hope that it will help the keener enthusiasts to plan their birding forays over a far wider area than just their local wildernesses. More and better observation and documentation of such reserves, and their living natural resources, will lead to greater public awareness and help mobilize the people's concern for their protection. Such observation is also the key to our understanding of natural systems, of the threats to them, and of ways to protect them.

### Sultanpur Lake Bird Sanctuary, Haryana

Only 50 km from Delhi, the Sultanpur Lake was once a popular shooting block of Haryana. In 1971 this one square km lake with a small area of surrounding thorn scrub forest was notified as a Sanctuary. Today there is a Wildlife Department office with a small library and a museum for the serious wildlifer and a Haryana Tourism Bar and Restaurant for the holiday maker, though I feel that the latter is more a bane than a facility, thanks to the disturbance created by the activities of unruly tourist groups.

The sanctuary area is a haven for birdwatchers and nature lovers. The lake is rainfed and the sanctuary comes to life after the monsoon when it fills up. A few species converge on the lake just before the monsoon rains begin, to nest in the heronries on the tiny islands in the middle of the water. These include the area's resident painted storks, egrets and herons. But the sanctuary's main attraction is in the arrival of its winter visitors. Ducks, geese, pelicans, flamingos, cormorants, sandpipers, demoiselle cranes, white ibis, spoonbills and a host of other waterbirds start settling in by late September and arrivals continue till December.

The best time to visit Sultanpur is winter (November to February) when the monsoon slush has dried sufficiently to permit walking along the trail on the lake's periphery, to observe or photograph birds and other wildlife. The area has a resident herd of nilgai and there are sporadic reports of blackbuck from the adjacent agricultural belt. The other life forms include hare, porcupine, snakes, lizards, turtles, and a variety of spiders and insects.

Since the lake and woodland areas are fairly small, birdwatching with binoculars is enjoyable at Sultanpur. But most of the waterbirds are too far to photograph satisfactorily without long lenses (400 mm and more). Nevertheless, there are a myriad species of other birds, smaller mammals and lesser life to watch and photograph.

Best Season: November to February.

Climate: Temperatures from 46°C to 5°C. Rainfall about 500 mm annually.

Facilities: Tourist huts; Wildlife Deptt. office, with a museum and library; Wildlife Guard available as Guide on prior intimation.

Approach: By road—Delhi 50 km, Gurgaon 15 km. Nearest railhead — Gurgaon 15 km.

Information: Wildlife Officer, Kothi No. 971, Sector 9, Panchkula, Distt. Ambala, Haryana.

### Keoladeo Ghana National Park, Bharatpur, Rajasthan

Late in the 19th century, the Maharaja of Bharatpur felt that he could develop the Keoladeo marsh — at that time a small patch of scrub forest around a shrine of Shiva, with a rainfed depression — into a prime habitat for waterfowl and make it his shooting preserve. So he had small dams and dykes built to harvest rainwater as well as the waters of the Gambhiri and the Banganga rivers. The result of this manipulation was the Keoladeo Ghana of today — Asia's finest, and best known, waterbird habitat.

Keoladeo was notified as a Sanctuary in 1956 and as a National Park in 1981. Recognizing its global conservation importance, UNESCO has designated Keoladeo as a World Heritage site. This 29 sq km area has about 1,100 hectares of marsh habitat, surrounded by a fine scrub forest. Motorable embankments divide the sanctuary into compartments. Trees growing on these embankments, as well as those submerged in the water, provide excellent perching, roosting and heronry sites for the waterbirds. Over 120 bird species are resident in this area and breed here regularly. The sanctuary hosts hundreds of migrant species each winter and nearly 350 species of resident and migratory birds have been recorded here. Keoladeo is the last surviving wintering ground in India of the endangered Siberian cranes. A gradually diminishing number of these birds has been arriving each successive winter, from their breeding grounds 6400 km away in Siberia.

The bird diversity of Keoladeo includes various species of storks, cranes, ibises, cormorants, ducks and geese, waders, plovers, kingfishers, rollers, bee-eaters, raptors, scavengers, owls, songbirds, pelicans, herons, pigeons and doves, partridges and a profusion of grassland and scrub birds. The surrounding forest has wild boar, chital, sambhar, nilgai, blackbuck, mongoose, otter, python, monitor lizard, jungle cat, fishing cat, jackal, fox, porcupine, and hare. The marshes abound in fish life, water snakes, turtles, and amphibians.

The best way to observe and photograph the heronries and waterbirds at Bharatpur is to take an early morning ride in one of the Park's punt boats. Hired bicycles and cycle rickshaws, with a band of rickshaw pullers trained in bird identification, are equally rewarding though with these vehicular conveniences you tend to cover more of the ground species and raptors. Nest sites and specific situations can be covered best if you are on your own, or with a willing forest guard as guide. Private motor vehicles are not allowed in the sanctuary and you should be prepared for a lot of walking on beautifully wooded embankments and through some exciting patches of forest.

Best Season: October to March for migratory waterfowl, Siberian crane, waders and larger waterbirds such as pelican and flamingo; late monsoon for heronries and nesting of storks, egrets and herons.

Climate: Temperatures range from 49°C to 2°C. Rainfall about 650 mm. Peak summer is arid and dusty; winter days are sunny and nights damp and cold. Winter mornings are foggy and chilly.

Facilities: ITDC Forest Lodge, Forest Deptt. Rest House and log hut inside the Park; Rajasthan Tourism Saras Lodge and the Golbagh Palace Hotel just outside; other accommodation in Bharatpur town (2-5 km); boating facility available on booking; Forest Guards and trained rickshaw pullers as guides; bicycles on hire; no catering except for a tea kiosk for day visitors; lodges have catering for room occupants.

Approach: By road—Delhi 176 km, Agra 50 km; Nearest railhead — Bharatpur 5 km; airport — Agra 55 km.

Information: Deputy Chief Wildlife Warden, Keoladeo National Park, Bharatpur, Rajasthan.

## Chilika Lake Sanctuary, Orissa

Covering 900 sq km of lake, shore and lagoon habitat, the Chilika Sanctuary is part of a 1,100 sq km lagoon system separated from the Bay of Bengal by a sandbar. It was notified as a Sanctuary in 1973. Chilika is India's largest saltwater lake, and one of the country's six wetlands listed under the international Ramsar Convention.

Chilika is one of the largest wintering quarters and stopovers for migratory birds in India. Huge flocks start arriving in late October to stay on till March. Several species of waders, raptors and shore birds are resident throughout the year. Among the notable species of the area are flamingos, barheaded geese, several varieties of ducks, gulls, terns, plovers, osprey, white-bellied sea eagle, waders, pelicans and herons.

The best spots for observing and photographing birds in Chilika are its sandbars and small islands scattered in the lake. These, as well as the lagoon where dolphins can be occasionally seen, are approachable by boats, available on hire from the tourist complex at Rambha.

Best Season: October to March

Facilities: Rest Houses and Tourist Lodges at Rambha, Barkul and Balugaon.

Approach: By road — Bhubaneswar town 70 km; Nearest town— Balugaon 1 km; Railhead — Balugaon 1 km; Airport—Bhubaneswar 100 km.

Information: Divisional Forest Officer, Ghunar South, P O Khurda, Puri Distt, Orissa.

## Nelapattu Sanctuary, Andhra Pradesh

An old and large heronry of the Nelapattu village, this 4.5 sq km area was established as a Sanctuary in 1976. In winter the village tank comes alive with several species of migratory and local birds.

Best Season: November to March

Facilities: PWD Rest House at Sulurpetta.

Approach: Nearest town — Sulurpetta 16 km; Railhead — Dorwai Satramm 1 km; Airport — Madras 120 km.

Information: Additional Conservator of Forests (Wildlife Management), Sulurpetta, Nellore Distt, Andhra Pradesh.

## Ranganathittoo Bird Sanctuary, Karnataka

Sixteen km north of Mysore, this Sanctuary comprises a number of small islands in the Kaveri river. There are mixed heronries on these islands, which come to life in June with the first nesting activity. The nesting trees can be approached by boats available on hire. Bird species of the area include openbilled stork, white ibis, little egret, darter, cattle egret, cormorant, pond heron, river tern and spoonbill. There are a few crocodiles in the river, too.

A 27 sq km area of this river and its islands was notified as a Sanctuary in 1940. Just 10 km away are the ruins of Srirangapatnam, the historic capital of Tipu Sultan.

Best Season: June to October

Facilities: One guest house; boats for hire; observation tower.

Approach: By road — Mysore 16 km; Railhead and Airport—Mysore 16 km; Bangalore 110 km.

Information: Additional Conservator of Forests (Wildlife Preservation), Vanivilas Road, Mysore-4, Karnataka.

## Vedanthangal Sanctuary, Tamil Nadu

Vedanthangal has had a long history of conservation. In 1798 it saw what was perhaps India's oldest legislation for bird protection, in the form of a shooting prohibition. It is a tiny village tank with waterlogged trees and a grove around it, which serve as a mixed heronry for a variety of water birds. Several species are resident and breeding, and many more are winter visitors.

Best Season: October to February.

Facilities: One Rest House.

Approach: By road — Madras 80 km; nearest town— Maduranthakam 15 km; Rail—Maduranthakam 15 km; Chingleput 28 km; Airport — Meenambakkam (Madras) 70 km.

Information: Wildlife Warden, 50 IV Main Road, Gandhi Nagar, Madras-600020, Tamil Nadu.

# Birdwatching and Photography

Observing birds and recording data about them is not merely a discipline of ornithology; it is also a highly rewarding hobby and leisure-time pursuit, capable of giving lifelong pleasure and deep satisfaction to amateurs as well as professionals. Over the past few decades, birdwatching has acquired immense popularity in several countries, including India, and specialized ornithological and birdwatching excursions are now offered at many places.

For an absolute novice, birdwatching can begin with things as simple as observing and identifying birds in the immediate neighbourhood and learning some interesting facts about them. This interest, once aroused, forms the very basis of serious bird study, including photodocumentation, sound recording, sketching or painting, bird counts and censuses; and to a more formal, academic or professional involvement with ornithological work.

One does not have to go far to begin birdwatching. Several species of birds will be living around the house, in the nearby garden, by a canal or pond close to your residence, and in the woodland just beyond. Birds are found even in the most crowded and noisy concrete jungles. For most beginners the only equipment needed is a pair of good binoculars, a good guidebook, and a notebook. It is extremely important, however, even for the amateur, to be sincere and systematic in his approach.

For really satisfying and systematic study, one must visit a variety of habitats within reach, periodically and regularly over the whole year, eg. seashore cliffs, rocks, beaches, sand banks of rivers, tidal flats, marshes, lagoons, lakes, ponds, streams, scrub/thorn bushes, thickets and hedges, wastelands. grassy meadows, lone trees, groves, orchards, fruiting/flowering trees, forests, parks, gardens, lawns, farms and forested hills and bare slopes. Try to locate and record nests, perches and favourite feeding areas and times, watering points and song posts. Listen carefully, memorise and differentiate between contact calls, warning calls, alarms and songs. Quite often bird sounds help in detecting the presence of birds before sighting them visually and in many confusingly similar birds, sounds are more definitive indicators for identification.

One begins by becoming familiar with the area one is going to birdwatch in and with its avian diversity. Of course, on an unplanned excursion this may not be possible. For a general overview of birds in India and its various regions, it is best to read one or more of the several excellent bird books. Some of these are listed in the Bibliography. There are also a few good magazines on Indian wildlife. Most of them devote considerable space to birds and birdwatching.

The best approach, however, is to develop an association with local, regional or national societies of naturalists. The advantages of doing this are many. Working in isolation, it is nearly impossible to cross-check the accuracy or veracity of one's observations. There are many societies and associations doing commendable work with amateur ornithologists in India. Some of them have journals which provide a veritable goldmine of information on the birds of the region. Serious work requires access to books, journals and checklists. It is neither always feasible, nor advisable, to acquire everything personally, but one can always borrow equipment or exchange information, if one has links with local groups or individuals with a similar interest.

A few tips about the equipment and other fieldgear. Good binoculars are necessary if one intends to do something more than gaze at birds. For amateur work, magnifications of between 6 x 30 and 8 x 40 will generally suffice. More powerful binoculars, say 10 x 50 or 12 x 50, are helpful when observing smaller species from a distance. Spotting telescopes with magnifications of 16x or 20x, mounted on tripods, are necessary for those interested in studying nesting behaviour, waders, or waterbirds on distant sheets of water.

One ought to wear earth colours for field work. Bright colours themselves do not necessarily alarm birds, but one's presence is given away quicker and then birds become wary, either staying in hiding or keeping a greater distance than they would normally do. It is known that two human features — the head and shoulder outline, and the bipedal stance — are alien to animals and birds and arouse instinctive fear. Therefore, serious wildlifers contrive to conceal themselves fully or at least these two features. I sometimes simply drape a green or khaki mosquito net over myself, after making a provision for limb movement.

Various types of hides have been designed and used by hunters and naturalists. The simplest is a canvas cubicle supported on sticks or a metal framework. One to three side may have portholes with flaps for sighting. There are numerous variations on this basic design: standing hides, sitting hides, roofed or roofless hides, collapsible frame hides, zip-up hides and so on. You can prepare an inexpensive, portable hide with the help of gunny bag material, with irregular green and brown cloth patches and strips stitched on the outer side, and using four sticks. Paint, instead of cloth patches, will do equally well. Four additional cross sticks may be tied if one wants it to be a semi-permanent structure, although this reduces the hide's wrap-and-carry convenience. This type of hide is suitable for observing birds from the ground, but some sort of a *machan* is a must if one intends making observations from high up in a tree.

Whichever hide one chooses or fabricates, it must be functional, comfortable and equipped for a prolonged stay. An ideal hide is waterproof, well ventilated, roomy enough for movement, have pegs or pockets for hanging equipment, and peepholes with closable flaps at both sitting and standing heights, preferably in all directions. Small items such as a stool or a folding chair, a water bottle, some refreshments, a towel, mosquito repellent, etc. may appear to be luxuries, but when one actually starts using a hide extensively, one soon realizes their worth. A closed car or jeep can make an excellent observation hide. Birds of the open country, particularly those found in the vicinity of roads with traffic, treat closed vehicles as natural objects. So long as one stays inside the vehicle without sticking out parts of the body, most birds will remain at ease and allow prolonged observation from close quarters.

However, if one cannot, or does not wish to, encumber oneself with a hide, there are simple field techniques one should employ to cause as little distraction or alarm to the birds as is possible. Break the head outline by wearing a floppy cap with a wide brim. This will also cut out the glare when looking into the bright sky, and keep the head cool in summer and warm in the winter. Needless to say, choose a dull, earth colour. Wherever possible, stand or crouch behind vegetation or a tree bole, so that the legs are hidden. Make no sudden or jerky movement, and ensure that companions observe the same rules. Talk only in low tones (whispering does not help actually, because whispers carry far). And avoid making clinking sounds if there is metal or hard plastic in the equipment. Wear the same, or similar coloured, outfit each day in the field. This helps to get the resident birds and animals of the study area accustomed to one's appearance and presence. Let them judge the watcher's harmless intentions, by not making an early attempt at approaching them, their nests or the young too close. In any case, one must not touch or otherwise disturb bird nests, eggs or young.

If one chances upon a baby bird that has dropped out of its nest, simply put it back in place if one can locate and reach the nest. Contrary to popular belief, parent birds do not reject their young just because they have been handled by humans. If one cannot locate or reach the nest, place the baby carefully on a branch or the top of a shrub beyond the reach of a cat or a dog. Its hunger calls will soon attract the parents and they will feed and guard it. It is extremely difficult to ensure the survival of unfledged chicks if they are brought home, since the nature of their food, the frequency and intensity of feeding, their hygiene requirements and, above all, their need for parental warmth and brooding, are nearly impossible to replicate. Faced with such a situation, the best course is to overcome emotion and contact one's birdwatching circle for help in locating a suitable facility—a bird hospital or an experienced birdkeeper. Till such time as the young bird is in safe hands, one may have to keep it warm, dry and frequently fed on juicy worms, as these are a safe bet for most bird babies; any trials with other food may kill the bird, unless one knows its diet and feeding method.

Early morning is the best time for observing birds, as it is the peak of activity and vocalization for most of the species living on the ground, in shrubbery and in trees. Some of the night foragers can also be seen returning to their resting places in the morning. Although in wooded areas the raptors are not hunting in the early morning—their feathers are usually a little damp from the dew of the previous night—they can be seen fairly frequently, perched high on treetops or poles, trying to catch the first rays of the sun to get crisp, while they scan the countryside for potential prey. In fact, one should take advantage of such activity patterns of birds to schedule the day and cover as many habitats as possible. Use the early morning to go to a wetland or marsh where the birds will be active, move to the surrounding woodland as the sun comes up and use the later part of the morning to watch the day feeders out in the fields. In coastal areas and on the larger water sheets, bird activity continues nearly all day long. Late afternoon and evening are ideal for observing crepuscular species such as night herons, owls and nightjars, and to observe the daytime feeders, such as cranes and some ducks and geese, returning after feeding in the fields.

In the West, birdwatchers frequently use tape recordings of bird sounds to attract birds in the field and also for making comparisons with their observations. Some authors suggest the use of imitation of bird sounds or mimicked distress calls to attract birds. In India, however, I am not aware of anyone having made serious use of either method for bird study. Tape recordings of Indian birds are not available in India as they are in some Western countries, and the average Indian birdwatcher does not have access to the gadgetry needed for such recordings. As to the second method of mimicked distress calls, its efficacy is proven from the good old days of duck shoots; you only have to ask an experienced hunter, or in our age, a poacher about it.

It is extremely important to gather data in a thorough way, adopting wherever possible standard terms and units and standardized methodologies, if you are aware of them. I have found the following standard form devised by the British Trust for Ornithology quite useful.

1. Name of birdwatcher.
2. Name of any birdwatcher accompanying you on the sortie.
3. Site or location of observations — refer to well known landmarks.
4. Date of observation—mention times at which observations were made and the percentage of the total area covered during the sortie.
5. Data gathered: type of vegetation, weather conditions—cloud cover, temperature, wind, rain, visibility, etc.; environmental features — type of terrain: rock, stony, gravel or scree, coarse sand, fine sand, mud or ooze, clay, humus, peat, etc; sloping or otherwise, presence of surface water expanses or other water source, man-made buildings or other structures nearby, etc.
6. List of species observed — for each species indicate the number of different sightings made; if possible make notes of the sex of the individuals sighted, the sighting with the largest number of

individuals observed together and the approximate number of individuals seen or present in the area; all the various observations about behaviour and other features that you consider worth mentioning.

For identification the following points need careful observation and recording:—

(a) Size — comparing with the more common species like sparrow, mynah, crow, domestic fowl, geese, sarus.

(b) Colour — Overall colouration, associated colours, colour of pupil, any noteworthy pattern/patch/streaks/bars/spots on head, neck, breast, cheeks, wings, tail, beak, legs, and around the eyes, and moustachial streaks. Some colour patterns and other diagnostic features are visible only in flight.

(c) Shape and size of head, beak, tail, wings, legs, claws, spurs, crest, webbed feet, cover on legs.

(d) Behaviour—shy, bold, tame, neurotic, silent, strident, fidgety, flitting, gregarious, loner, pairs, groups, flocks,pugnacious, sexes in mixed groups or isolated.

(e) Flight pattern—straight, undulating, take off and landing, zigzagging, spiralling, wing beating pattern and frequency.

(f) Surface movement—hopping, walking, running, waddling, swimming, dabbling, diving.

(g) Feeding method and food.

(h) Perching posture.

(i) Nest shape, material, location, construction, egg colour/pattern, size, numbers.

Such record keeping organizes one's data into a systematic format, makes it immediately utilizable, and comparable with available standard information. Note down what is observed, making definitive statements only when sure, keeping queries for later clarification by a more experienced birdwatcher or with the help of a manual. Use the concept of elimination to narrow down the identification of species. Beginning with a number of probables on the basis of general similarities, reject those that do not precisely match the description personally noted, with the help of the identification key in a field guide or handbook. Besides physical descriptions, use other observations such as location, season and time of sighting, any salient behavioural aspects, etc. to arrive at the correct identification. In the beginning one need not delve beyond recognizing the gross characteristics of Orders and Families. Use one or more authentic handbook or guide for identification. But a word of caution here. Confusion frequently results when one cross refers two guides, because these can differ on basic descriptions, and colour sketches actually do not agree for many species. A number of Indian productions suffer from inaccurate colour reproduction and poor drawing quality.

### Photography

Bird photography is a very challenging field and requires adequate knowledge of bird behaviour as well as of some special techniques of photography. It is not the scope of this book to teach the basics of photography. I wish, instead, to share with the reader some general information and some ideas based on my personal experience, accumulated over two decades of nature photography.

For reasons of economy, versatility and portability, the 35 mm single lens reflex (SLR) is the most suitable camera format for the wildlife photographer. Medium and large format cameras and lenses are too heavy for the field, besides their high costs and the limited range of optics and accessories. Autofocus and programmed cameras do have many advantages in some fast action situations. The auto exposure (AE) mode is certainly helpful in as much as it cuts down on the time taken in estimating exposure and reduces missed shots. But in the unusual light and shade conditions encountered in bird habitats—dark object against the sky or against a bright background, dappled light through foliage or a dark background with a small main object illuminated by angled light, and so on, the simple auto-exposure systems tend to go wrong and require manual corrections based on the photographer's experience. More advanced multi-pattern-segment (MPS) auto-exposure cameras are better equipped to deal with such situations.

Zoom lenses offer a compromise solution of the need to have several focal lengths to cover all distances, situations and bird sizes. Wide-angle to normal focal lengths (28-85 mm or 35-70 mm) are ideal for general habitat, large flocks and sunrise/sunset shots; short to medium telephoto/zoom lenses (60-300 mm, 70-200 mm, 80-210 mm, or single focal lengths from this range) for large birds at moderate distances; and long telephoto lenses (400 mm upwards, to possibly 1000 mm) are essential for small birds and long-distance coverage. There is a whole new range of compact telephoto lenses with mirror optics available these days, but they have severely limited depths of field and no aperture adjustment. As a result one has limited control over exposure time. Tele-extenders or converters boost the focal length to give a larger image size, but the resultant losses in sharpness and brightness are serious handicaps. If one can find a 1.5x or 2x converter with reasonably good optics (sharpness, flatness of field), one should be able to put it to good use, at least in brightly lit situations.

A strong flash is useful in lighting nest holes and birds in deep shade or foliage, or as fill-in. A sturdy tripod is a must for those wishing to set up at one spot for long sessions. Its use is recommended while shooting with long lenses, to avoid pictures with blur. A good tripod should have well placed, smooth operating controls for elevation, tilting, swiveling and locking. It should be able to take the combined weight of camera body, long lens, motor drive and tele converter, without wobbling. But if a tripod is not available, one can still hand-hold long lenses by perfecting one's breathing and camera holding techniques to minimize camera shake. Use a rigid support — tree trunk, wall, car or box—to brace oneself against or to place the camera on. Practice the postures, grip and shutter release techniques recommended by the camera manual and photographic guides. Do not shoot from inside a vehicle if the engine is running. Even otherwise the vehicle body is unstable, particularly if there are other occupants in it.

If possible keep an additional manual camera body, which takes the same range of lenses and accessories, but is free of the shortcomings of the auto/electronic (jamming on battery failure, exposure goof-ups in tricky lighting situations, vulnerability to vibrations, heat, cold, etc.). Motor drives or autowinders have a definite advantage in fast action situations and in remote control photography. Similarly, remote cables, sensors and radio/infrared beams and photo-electric trigger devices are extremely useful in the photo documentation of fast action, flight, or where the photographer cannot position or hide himself. The list of add-ons is long but while each of these has a definite advantage to offer, one must decide what to have, based on one's requirement, intended use of the photographic output, and budget.

Among other fieldgear needed is a camera bag that is waterproof, dustproof, cushioned, lockable, crushproof, designed for easy access to its contents and preferably an earth colour. One should also carry a cleaning kit consisting of a soft blower brush, or lens tissue, a clean lint-free wiping cloth and some lens cleaning fluid. Always keep a spare set of batteries and enough extra film, because there are no replacements out in the field.

One can use black and white, colour negative, or colour transparency film. The choice will be entirely governed by one's personal liking for a particular medium (for instance some photographers find black and white more exciting) and the ultimate use one intends to put the pictures to. If the intention is to use them for presentations, publication or educational work, then the best medium is colour slide film. But if one desires to build up personal albums or portfolios, one may prefer colour or black and white negative film, from which enlargements can be made to specifications. The choice of film speeds depends on the nature of work. For general habitat or bird pictures, using the camera on a tripod in bright daylight, film speeds of 50, 64 or 100 ASA/ISO are very good. To freeze fast action as well as for hand-held long lenses, or for dim light situations, faster film speeds of 160, 200 or 400 ASA/ISO are required. Of course, the fineness of picture grain — and therefore reproduction quality — declines as film speed increases. So one has to strike a balance, using one's own judgement.

Now for a few practical hints. Check your equipment periodically, especially for signs of attack by dust, moisture, grit, fungus or battery fluid. If your equipment travels a lot with you, check occasionally for screws and other fasteners getting loose by vibration, and tighten them gently. You may apply small drops of non-corrosive adhesive (or nail lacquer) on the exposed screwheads which will prevent the screws from coming loose. Protect your equipment from motor vibration and bumps by cushioning various items with pieces of sponge or bubble-packaging material. Carry it on your lap or on a well padded seat during vehicle rides; never place camera bags on the floor of the aircraft or vehicle or in the luggage boot. Do not place film or equipment in the glove compartment or on the dashboard of a car because these heat up excessively. In the field, store all your gear in the shade and out of harm's way. Whenever handling a camera, make it a habit to first put the strap around your neck. If you ever happen to drop it, this will prevent it from falling to the ground.

The selection of subject matter is essentially a personal choice, at least for amateurs. Some are turned on by the ferocity and power of raptors, others by colour

and patterns of plumage, still others seek rare or endangered species. But most prefer general photo-coverage according to opportunity and availability of the subjects. Having once decided on the subject, study guidebooks and other literature to know the when (season, time) and where (location, habitat) of the selected species. These are the same factors to bear in mind as discussed earlier for birdwatching.

Observe the activities of the subjects to establish patterns based on their habits, routines and natural cycles. Learn to anticipate events and movements of birds, instead of chasing them all over for 'pot shots'. Practise pre-focusing at spots where one expects the birds to arrive. For example, a woodpecker will usually climb a tree in spirals, so focus where it can be expected to emerge next from behind the tree trunk; similarly, locate favoured perches, songposts, trees in fruit, flowers with nectar, entrances to nest holes, water points (especially in arid regions) and so on.

Nondescript pictures have little use; they waste photographic material and block money. So learn to be selective and critical in your shooting. If you are doing portraits, snap when the bird has a pleasing posture. Choose an aperture for a depth of field adequate to get at least the bird's head and eyes (and preferably the diagnostic features as well) in sharp focus. Eyes should be well lit, so that they have what photo editors call 'catchlight'. In action photography, press the trigger a fraction of a second before the peak action, so that the shot can actually capture that moment. Use flash to fill in and soften harsh shadows; do not try to eliminate shadows altogether or the modelling effect will be lost. Take help from nature photography guides and existing picture portfolios of known bird photographers to develop an aesthetic sense of composition and framing. If planning to put the pictures to commercial use, practise bracketing of important shots, i.e. shooting a graded sequence of exposures, various depths of field or bird postures, so that a selector may exercise choice.

There is a great need for accurate photographic documentation of Indian birds, both for publication and for the scientific study of all aspects of bird life: nest building, incubation, feeding, flight, courtship, populations, threats to survival, conservation status, and so on. The whole world of birds is waiting out there, to be observed, photographed and documented. So have a field day birdwatching and shooting and, while you are at it, have fun!

Magpie robin

Pelicans

**Pelicans**
Like a team of cooperative fishermen, a pelican flock surrounds a shoal of fish and drives them to the shallows, to scoop them up in their pouches. Flock movement in water is extremely well synchronised, like a flotilla turning, wheeling, advancing, and reversing in unison. When not feeding, they float gracefully on the water, preening their feathers with secretion from their oil glands, or just resting their heavy bills on their backs, like this white pelican (*Pelecanus onocrotalus*).

Despite their enormous size, pelicans are effortless fliers and frequently soar on thermals, in the company of vultures and storks.

Little cormorant

**Cormorant**
Cormorants are experts at diving and swimming. They live exclusively off fish, which they catch underwater, sometimes with team effort. Like darters, cormorants also do not have any oil glands and so they must perch frequently in sunny spots, and spread their feathers to dry after a session in the water.

Besides the little cormorant (*Phalacrocorax niger*) shown here, we have also the large cormorant (*P. carbo*) and the Indian shag (*P. fuscicollis*). The pattern on the feathers, as seen in this bird, develops only during the breeding phase.

**Darter**
Anyone who sees a darter (*Anhinga rufa*) swimming underwater, with only its long sinuous neck above the surface, can easily mistake it for a snake. For this peculiar habit the darter is also called the snakebird. Its neck has a larger number of vertebrae than in other birds, and is equipped with special muscles that can shoot the beak forward like a harpoon.

Hunting individually, a darter spears its prey — chiefly fish but occasionally amphibians and even snakes — underwater; then surfaces to jerk its neck backwards and tosses the prey up in the air; as it falls the bird catches it in its open beak and gulps it down, head first. If the fish is large, it is bashed to facilitate swallowing.

Darters spend long periods grooming themselves, combing their feathers with their bills and removing fluff and debris from them. They also need to spread out their wings after a spell in the water, to dry them. Both sexes develop a few elongated feathers on the back during the breeding season.

Darter

Pond heron in its breeding plumage

Pond heron (winter plumage)

Pond heron fishing

**Pond Heron**

Also known as the paddybird, *Ardeola grayii* is a common heron wherever there is enough water with small prey — fish, frogs, crabs, insects, etc. It can be seen even by roadside ditches and drains. It stands patiently hunched up at the water's edge, jabbing to catch unwary prey. Pond herons are usually solitary but associate with other species during roosting and nesting. Their nests are made amidst mixed heronries in large trees, often in the middle of a village.

Generally inconspicuous because of their dull colours, pond herons in flight attract attention with flashes of the brilliant white of their underwings. During the summer months paddybirds appear in their breeding plumage, with beautiful crests and plumes drooping down their backs and heads.

**Grey Heron**

This denizen of shallow lagoons, lakes, marshes, and forest ponds is more active during dawn and dusk hours, spending the larger part of the day hunched up in a tree or under bushes overlooking water. When hunting, it wades through shallow water seemingly aimlessly, but keeps a sharp lookout and grabs the unwary fish or frog passing within striking distance. It is a wary and vigilant bird, and a solitary hunter.

Grey herons (*Ardea cinerea*) make usually large nests of sticks and twigs in trees isolated from other heronries. Sometimes the nests may be placed low amidst reedbeds in the water. The unfledged chicks have dirty grey down and the parents feed them on regurgitated food.

Grey heron

Grey heron with young

Little bittern

**Little Bittern**

A typical hunchbacked cousin of the pond heron, the little bittern (*Ixobrychus minutus*) is a solitary skulker seen hiding among reedbeds, water hyacinths, or lily leaves. Otherwise similar to the pond heron in general and feeding habits, this bittern displays a wonderful concealment behaviour. When in fear of being discovered, the bird straightens out its neck and points its beak skywards, and in this posture it freezes, to blend perfectly with its surroundings.

Night herons on the nest

**Night Heron**
After resting all day in shady trees, colonies of night herons (*Nycticorax nycticorax*) stir to life at dusk. In ones and twos, the herons fly out with 'kwaark' calls and spread out to feed all night in ponds, inundated fields, shallow lagoons, etc. In sharp contrast to the other herons' habit of waiting silently, night herons actively catch fish, crabs, frogs, and insects. They fly back to their roosting trees before the day gets bright.

Night herons have striking ruby-red eyes and white plumes dropping from their black crests, which make them pleasing subjects for bird photographers despite their skulking behaviour.

Night heron

Egrets

Cattle egret

**Egrets**

Egrets in India have two main breeding seasons, June to August in the North and November to March in the South. Their nests are shallow twig platforms built in trees, sometimes near villages and not necessarily near water. Most species lay 3-6 eggs and incubate them for about 4 weeks. The chicks, which are reared in the nest for about 30 days, are prolific eaters and keep both parents busy hunting for food. All egrets feed their chicks on regurgitated food.

In their breeding phase all egrets bear ornamental, snow-white plumes on their heads, backs, and tails. The huge demand in the West for these 'aigrettes', for use in fashionable headgear, nearly led to the wipe out of egrets in many countries. It took several years before conservationists were able to build up public concern and pressure to get the trade outlawed.

All egrets share their nesting colonies with other heron species, cormorants, and darters. The bird shown in this picture is in its breeding plumage, with bright orange breast and bill.

**Cattle Egret**

Primarily a bird of the marshes and grasslands, the cattle egret (*Bubulcus ibis*) has spread over vast regions due to the expansion of agriculture. To its diet of frogs, lizards, and insects it adds a whole range of agricultural pests and cattle parasites. Cattle egrets can be seen attending on grazing cattle and ridding them of their parasites, or catching insects and small reptiles disturbed by workers, tractors, or animals in the fields. It is fascinating how these birds have adapted to the advent of heavy machines on agricultural lands and follow them fearlessly. In fact, they treat them as providers of food!

Median egrets

**Median Egret**
Distinguishablc from the little egret by its dull yellow, black-tipped bill and by the absence of a crest in its breeding plumage, this egret (*Egretta intermedia*) occurs in the same habitat as the former and often in mixed colonies, in association with several other species of herons and cormorants. In the breeding phase the yellow beak becomes black.

**Little Egret**
This gregarious snow-white bird (*Egretta garzetta*) is widely distributed over marshes, lakes, ponds, and tidal flats. Its nests are made among mixed heronries, where it associates with other species. Flocks often invade flooded rice paddies to catch prawns, frogs, small fish, and reptiles.

Little egret

White storks

**White Storks**

Storks do not just bring babies. There is an ancient fable in Sweden that describes the crucifixion of Jesus Christ. According to it, the stork was aggrieved by the event. It circled around the crucified Christ and cried 'Styrka! Styrka!' ('Strength! Strength!'). Since then, it has been revered as sacred. An ancient Egyptian seal depicts a farmer with a harnessed stork ploughing the field with its bill.

In the Indian countryside, too, storks benefit from the religious sentiment of villagers and are not harmed. They are too many good things rolled into one. They symbolize long life and marital harmony (the same pair can be seen for years). They are the farmer's friends because they destroy pests such as locusts and mice. And they have a welcome, benevolent presence.

The white storks (*Ciconia ciconia*) shown here are winter visitors, but there are six other storks resident and breeding in India. They are the painted stork (*Mycteria leucocephala*), blacknecked stork (*Ephippiorhynchus asiaticus*), whitenecked stork (*Ciconia episcopus*), openbilled stork (*Anastomus oscitans*), adjutant stork (*Leptoptilos dubius*), and the lesser adjutant (*Leptoptilos javanicus*).

The only vocalization a stork can produce is during its first few weeks when, as a hungry chick in the nest, it emits a call not unlike that of a crying human infant, to beg its parents for food or to attract their attention when they are away from the nest. But sometime during growth, the vocal cords become non-functional, rendering the stork completely mute. Adult storks, therefore, make no sounds except bill clattering. Their displays consist of unison clattering, throwing up their heads in synchronization, and circling their partners with outstretched wings.

Whitenecked stork

White storks, courtship behaviour

Adjutant stork

**Adjutant Stork**
The adjutant stork (*Leptoptilos dubius*) is an ungainly bird with a look of suspicion and disgust at the whole world. It is a shaggily built, heavy, bird with a huge bill and the neck usually has a hanging pouch, whose function is not authentically known although various properties have been attributed to it, including temperature regulation, ventilation, resonance (strange, since the bird is mute), food storage and so on. Adjutants are so named because of the military gait with which they walk about. The bird is actually more a scavenger than an eater of fish, frogs or reptiles. It can be seen milling around with vultures and other scavengers at garbage dumping sites and carcasses.

Painted storks mating

**Painted Stork**

The most familiar among the Indian storks is the painted stork (*Mycteria leucocephala*). Large breeding colonies form in tall trees at wetland sites just after the monsoon and there is hectic nest-building activity, with frequent quarrels over nesting material and elbow space. But painted storks are more generally seen as placid birds, wading knee deep through the waters of ditches and marshes, with their yellow bills open to grab at anything moving underneath. Sometimes a stork will shade an area of water under its wings. Whether it does so to cut out the reflection of the sky or to locate its prey by alarming it is not known. Parent birds frequently assume this posture to shade eggs or young in the nest.

Painted stork bringing nest material

Painted stork fishing

Painted stork colony

Painted stork pair in courtship

**Openbilled Stork**
The openbilled stork (*Anastomus oscitans*) has a uniquely adapted bill, for a specialized diet. It feeds on the large water snails found commonly in freshwater bodies. Its stout bill is convexly curved like a huge nutcracker, so it can easily crack open the mollusc shells and get at the juicy flesh.

Blacknecked stork

**Blacknecked Stork**
Blacknecked storks (*Ephippiorhynchus asiaticus*) have an interesting dimorphism. While both sexes are alike in all other respects, the eyes of the female are orange-yellow but those of the male are deep brown.

The blacknecked stork is yet another bird that is rapidly declining as a result of the destruction and diversion of India's wetlands. Since, however, it was never too common and is usually seen singly, its plight seems to go unnoticed. Like other storks, it is a heavy bird, requiring large quantities of fish, especially when it has young in the nest. Unfortunately, unlike the others, it cannot adapt to cramped conditions, being highly territorial. It prefers large *jheels*, marshes, and rivers.

Openbilled stork

White ibis colony

Glossy ibis

**Spoonbills and Ibises**

Closely related to the storks, ibises can be easily distinguished from a distance by their downcurved bills. The glossy ibis (*Plegadis falcinellus*) looks blackish from a distance but on closer observation the plumage reveals its brilliant copper, green, and purple tints. Some adults also have a blue-green sheen in their non-breeding phase. This ibis is often seen fishing in large groups at marshes and inundated grounds including fields.

More frequently seen, the white ibis (*Threskiornis melanocephalus*) is a white bird with a blackish, bald, head and neck. Gregarious like the glossy ibis, it also frequents shallow water bodies to catch its prey of fish, frogs, worms, and soft-bodied molluscs.

Spoonbill

The crested snow-white bird perched alongside this white ibis is a spoonbill (*Platalea leucorodia*), unmistakable because of its broad, spoon-shaped bill which it uses to sift food from shallow waters by wading in and sweeping the mud and water in semicircular motions of the bill. A sociable bird, it forms flocks of up to fifty and freely associates with other marsh birds. Its nesting colonies are also built among large mixed heronries, but sometimes entire colonies of spoonbill nests may also be seen.

Spoonbill and White ibis

Blacknecked grebe male

**Grebes**

Grebes are a small family of swimming and diving birds related to the ducks. While the dabchick — the smallest of our swimming birds — is quite common in water bodies throughout India, two rare species breed in the high Himalayan lakes and marshes during the summer, coming down to spend the winter in jheels and other large water sheets of North and North Western India. One of these is the blacknecked grebe (*Podiceps nigricollis*), a small and dumpy bird like the dabchick. During the breeding season it grows prominent golden 'eartufts'. The other is the great crested grebe (*Podiceps cristatus*), a duck sized version of the dabchick but with a long, slender neck and a prominent crest and 'eartufts' during the breeding season.

Grebes subsist on small frogs, crustaceans, and aquatic insects, which they catch by diving under water. The chicks seem to enjoy racing on the surface of the water and the young can often be seen riding on their parents' backs. They have a strange habit of gulping down their own feathers. According to some ornithologists this is done to aid digestion.

Great crested grebe

**Flamingo**

A flight of flamingos is a breathtaking sight. Wavy ribbons of scarlet float against a blue sky as the birds fly in V formations, occasionally drifting into a diagonal single file. Their courtship rituals are a joy to watch. They spread their wings and fold them as if curtseying on stage, twisting and bending their long necks backwards, encircling a wing and bending forward before the grand finale of flashing their wings, holding them above the neck as if saluting.

Flamingos have a unique filter feeding mechanism in their bills, that allows them to scoop up the bottom mud from shallow waters and sift it through the sieves in their upper beaks. They are thus able to occupy a special feeding niche — shallow bottom mud — and get their food — worms, larvae, crustaceans, and seeds of marsh plants.

They breed in large nesting colonies, called flamingo 'cities', which consist of hundreds of crowded conical mounds of sun-dried mud. A slight depression on top of each nest holds one or two bluish white eggs. Both parents participate in brooding. When the flock goes away to feed, the nursery is guarded by a few adults.

India seems to be losing its last flamingo 'city', in the Great Rann of Kachchh. Due to disturbances in the extremely fragile ecosystem of the Rann, the resident flamingos (*Phoenicopterus roseus*) have abandoned large parts of their former nesting areas and their current breeding status within India is unclear. However, small to medium flocks continue to sporadically inhabit lakes, salt flats, estuaries, and lagoons throughout India.

Flamingos

Shovellers in flight

## Shovellers

Closely related to swans and geese, ducks have webbed feet and water-repellent plumage. The typical rounded duck-bill reaches its highest development and specialization in shovellers (*Anas clypeata*). The duck swims with its neck and bill outstretched, to skim floating matter off the water's surface and filter out minute animals with the help of its spatulate, comb-tooth-edged bill. It also 'up-ends' in shallow water to pick animal matter from the bottom mud.

Shovellers are winter migrants to India and are quite common and widespread over the entire sub-continent. They breed in Ladakh and in farther localities of North Asia.

Lesser whistling teal

## Lesser Whistling Teal or Whistling Duck

This small duck (*Dendrocygna javanica*) is commonly come upon in weed-infested ponds and lakes. It is largely a nocturnal feeder, flying out to flooded fields of rice and other crops. It grazes on tender shoots and grains, but also takes molluscs and small fish. Teals walk quite comfortably on swampy ground and are expert divers. The lesser whistling teal emits shrill whistles ('seasick-seasick') in flight, while on the water it is largely quiet, only grunting in surprise or alarm. It is a tree-nester.

## Common Teal

One of the earliest migratory ducks to arrive in India, the common teal (*Anas crecca*) is already with us by end-August. Arrivals go on till November and the teals spread out widely over their wintering quarters, the entire Indian subcontinent south of the Himalaya. They can be seen on large and small water bodies with muddy bottoms. The bird can be easily distinguished at a distance because of its beautifully sculpted chestnut head and a tricoloured wing bar, with bands of black, green, and buff.

Common teals are purely herbivorous, subsisting on tubers, sprouts, and seeds of aquatic vegetation; they occasionally invade rice paddies to 'graze' the grains.

Common teal transiting through Ladakh

Common teal male

Comb duck male

## Comb Duck

The Indian name for the comb duck (*Sarkidiornis melanotos*) is *Nakta*, deriving from the rounded comb on top of its bill, which is diagnostic. The structure occurs only in the male and swells to a bigger size during the breeding season.

*Naktas* occur in small flocks on *jheels* and ponds that have reed beds and also affect flooded paddies where they 'graze' rice.

Their food includes grains, succulent shoots, and floating vegetation, but they sometimes catch frogs and insects also.

This is one of the duck species that nest on trees. It uses natural hollows in trees standing in water, to lay up to 12 eggs.

**Spotbill Duck**

Unmistakable even at a distance, because of its bright yellow tipped bill that gave this duck (*Anas poecilorhyncha*) its name, the spotbill is perhaps our commonest resident duck. It lives and breeds on reedy *jheels* and ponds, often in the vicinity of bustling highways or villages.

Spotbills are largely surface feeders, grazing vegetable matter off the surface in lakes and ponds, or up-ending to pick food from the bottom in shallow waters. Nesting among reeds and other vegetation by the waterside, spotbills raise large broods of up to 12. Both parents guard the ducklings from predators, sometimes one parent using the 'lame duck' trick — pretending as if it is injured or drowning — to distract the enemy away while the other herds the brood into the safety of thick cover.

Spotbill duck

Spotbill ducks

Spotbill duck with young

**Brahminy Duck**

The *Surkhaab* of old literature, *Tadorna ferruginea* are also the famous Chakwa-Chakwi of grandma's tales. Winter visitors to peninsular India, they settle on riverbanks, lagoons, lakes, and marshes in small flocks. Groups can be seen grazing at the water's edge, walking around in a clownish goose-step, or basking. Besides their usual diet of vegetable matter, they also take crustaceans, molluscs, insects, and small reptiles. Adult males have a dark collar around the base of the neck.

Their nearest breeding grounds are in Ladakh and Tibet. Brahminy ducks are hole breeders, nesting in holes in cliffs, tall sandbanks or dunes. As many as 16 eggs have been reported from a single nest, but the more usual number is 6 to 8.

Brahminy duck taking off

A Pintail duck pair

**Pintail Duck (*Anas acuta*)**

The long pin feathers projecting from the tapering tail — which also give this duck its name — distinguish the male pintail even at a distance. The female, too, has a tapering tail ending in a distinct point, though it lacks the pin feathers.

Pintails are winter visitors throughout India and live on *jheels* with reedy vegetation. They are largely vegetarian and feed during the day, but may adapt to nocturnal feeding in disturbed habitats. Pintails display 'up-ending' behaviour while feeding in shallow waters. They float bottoms-up and stretch their necks under water to probe the bottom mud for plant food.

Its flesh being quite clean as a result of vegetarian habit, the pintail is highly sought after as a table bird and large numbers are taken in game shoots on *jheels*.

Barheaded goose

**Barheaded Goose**

The *Rajhans* of ancient Sanskrit literature, the bar-headed goose (*Anser indicus*) is a winter visitor to the plains of North and East India, sporadically visiting some parts of Central India. Flocks settle on sandy strips in the middle of large rivers, where they rest during the day. Towards dusk skeins rise in V-formations or in single file to raid crop fields, occasionally inflicting heavy damage on young shoots of gram, mustard, and wheat. When scarecrows and shooing off fail, many a farmer takes to the gun. In this region their only breeding sites are in Tibet and Ladakh. From May to September they nest beside high-altitude lakes. Like cranes, geese also form lasting and strong pair bonds.

**King Vulture**

Variously known as king vulture, Pondicherry vulture or black vulture (*Sarcogyps calvus*), it stands apart from all other vultures, because of its naked red head and neck, and red legs and thighs. The red head, white patches on thighs and breast, and a thin white band running the whole length of the wing ventrally, are clearly identifiable even from great distances.

The bird is a carrion eater and an extremely efficient scavenger. Its nesting sites may be commonly seen in tall trees on the outskirts of villages or in the open countryside. It is found all over India and up to 2,000 m in the Himalaya, above which the lammergeier and the Himalayan griffon replace it. The king vulture probably got its regal epithet from the ferocious look it has, because of its bloody red features. In a congregation of vultures and kites at a carcass, however, it turns out to be the most gutless of the scavengers. Maintaining a safe distance from the throng, it makes cautious approaches on finding an accessible part of the cadaver and scurries away with a morsel if it can; otherwise it meekly allows itself to be jostled out.

Like all vultures, it enjoys soaring on thermals or sailing up in the skies on motionless wings, often in the company of pelicans or storks, particularly adjutants, who also join it in scavenging at carcasses.

King vulture

Himalayan griffon vulture

**Himalayan Griffon Vulture**

Probably the largest bird in the Indian Himalaya, this species of griffon (*Gyps himalayensis*) has a large ruff of pale brown streaked with white and adults are sandy white or khaki on the back, with occasional dark specimens, instead of dirty brown as in other vultures. It is a denizen of the Himalaya, found from the Western to the Eastern range of the mountains, including Bhutan, Pakistan, and China, besides a few other ranges of Afghanistan, Tibet, and Turkestan. It tends to keep in the vicinity of areas where it can locate sick or dead animals, particularly grazing herds or pack animals. In the Himalayan remoteness, one usually sees these vultures alone or in twos and threes, soaring over the valleys and ridges and sometimes on the ground. But they congregate rapidly at carcasses, evidently converging from great distances, and finish off everything edible except the skeleton. The bird in this picture has just finished gorging at a carcass, which is why its pale buff head has become bloodied red.



Whitebacked vulture

Pariah kite

Red kite (imm)

Red kite

Black-winged kite (Himachal)

**Common Pariah Kite**

Since it is our commonest raptor and an established scavenger in the vicinity of man, *Milvus migrans* suffers the ignominy of being called a 'pariah'. In fact, 'brown kite' or just 'common kite' would be a more apt name. New Delhi is reputed to have the largest world population of this bird.

Easily identified because of its forked tail, it is a handsome reddish brown bird. An expert at flight manoeuvres, it makes dashing swoops through congested streets, avoiding obstructions with ease, and picks up scraps of food or small dead animals, even snatching food from the hands of the unwary. Whenever opportunity allows, it preys on lizards, rodents,and injured or young birds.

**Red Kite**

A closely related species, the red kite (*Milvus milvus*) has a restricted distribution in India, occurring only in the Western Himalaya. It has a much deeper forked tail than the common kite. In habits it resembles the former.

**Blackwinged Kite**

The blackwinged kite (*Elanus caeruleus*) is a graceful small kite, easily identified by its red eyes, a black patch on either shoulder, and black wing tips. It frequents the edges of light deciduous forest and scrubland, and open grasslands.

Apart from the kestrel, the blackwinged kite is perhaps the only other raptor that can hover stationary over a spot. This it does by facing into a light wind and balancing itself on quivering wing tips, thus staying aloft for as long as a couple of minutes. In this position, or from a perch, it scans the ground for movement of prey. On perceiving the presence of a quarry, it descends in short oblique glides to an aerial vantage position from where it can swoop or drop for the final rush, and carries the prey off in its talons. Back on a safe perch it will dismember the victim and eat it.

Brahminy kite

**Brahminy Kite**
The Brahminy kite (*Haliastur indus*) is found only in the vicinity of lakes, rivers, and harbours. The forest populations prey upon frogs, fish, snakes, and winged termites, also rarely picking up small birds or rodents. Those living near harbours or fishing villages, however, scavenge for castaway offal and scraps from garbage.

Brahminy kites nest towards the end of winter, in huge trees near water. One or two chicks are raised and both parents take part in nest duties.

**Longlegged Buzzard**
Like most other birds of prey, the longlegged buzzard (*Buteo rufinus*) has confusing differences between juvenile and adult plumages, and more than one colour phase, depending on age, sex, season, and location within its breeding or wintering habitat.

This large hawk breeds in the Himalaya and normally comes down to the dry plains of northern and north western India to spend the winter. But stragglers may be seen in the dry scrub tracts in all seasons. It soars majestically, revealing its white underparts and the black-tipped primaries of its broad wings. It perches on a vantage point before the sun gets harsh and scans the countryside for rodents, lizards, snakes, and locusts, swooping down on its prey and dismembering it on the ground.

Longlegged buzzard

**Crested Hawk Eagle**
With a most apt Hindustani name—Shah Baaz—the crested hawk eagle (*Spizaetus cirrhatus*) is an elegant, slender bird with a long narrow crest of feathers pointing behind the head. Like in most raptors, the female is larger. Found mostly solitary, or occasionally in pairs, it is chiefly a forest bird, keeping to the better wooded areas. More often heard than seen, this eagle has a very musical, long-drawn Whistling note. During the daylight hours it an be seen sitting camouflaged amidst the foliage of the top canopy of a tree, waiting to take an unwary prey by ambush. In areas where domestic fowl forage near forest villages, it takes a heavy toll of these. In wilder habitats it preys on junglefowl, pheasant, squirrel, hare, and small rodents.

Crested hawk eagle

Lesser spotted eagle

**Lesser Spotted Eagle**
Rather indistinguishable in the field from the greater spotted eagle and found in many confusing colour stages, the lesser spotted eagle (*Aquila pomarina*) can be occasionally encountered in the more open forests and edges of woodlands. It sometimes descends to the ground from its high perch to straddle and kill its prey, mainly rodents, injured or weak birds including nestlings, lizards, frogs etc. It also pirates the prey of other raptors such as kites, which it chases and threatens quite frequently.

Crested serpent eagle

**Crested Serpent Eagle**
In the better forested areas of the country, the crested serpent eagle (*Spilornis cheela*) is a familiar sight, most frequently noticed by its striking underwing pattern visible in overhead flight. On other occasions one may encounter it sitting high in the branches of some tall tree, scanning the forest floor or a clearing for likely prey — snakes and other reptiles, small mammals, and weak or young birds. The bird has a loose crest on the head, which it occasionally erects, particularly in alarm or when excited. On locating a prey animal, it glides down silently and straddles the victim with its wings, killing with its sharp talons and beak. If undisturbed, it may eat on the ground, otherwise it carries the prey into the safety of a tree.

Hobby (imm)

Kestrel male

**Hobby**
The bird in this picture is an immature specimen from the Central Asian race of hobby (*Falco subbuteo centralasiae*), one of the three races that are found more or less mixed in their distribution in India; a fourth race — the Burmese hobby — occurs in Assam and further eastwards through Manipur. The Central Asian race is resident in the Himalaya.

Hobbies are perfect miniatures of the peregrine falcon, both in appearance and general habits. Their preying activities are largely crepuscular. Early mornings and late evenings are also the best lit hours for observing or photographing them, high in the air or on their perches. They soar and swoop down on their prey just like the peregrines. One of the most unforgettable sights for a birdwatcher in Ladakh is a loose flock of half a dozen or more hobbies soaring over a valley, chasing and hawking grasshoppers, swifts or swallows, demonstrating a bewildering array of aerobatics.

**Kestrel**
The bird pictured here with its prey belongs to a race of kestrel (*Falco tinnunculus tinnunculus*) that is resident in the Himalaya and migrates southwards to spend the winter in the plains and peninsular India. A smaller and darker race (*Falco tinnunculus objurgatus*) is resident in South-West India and Sri Lanka.

Falconers consider the kestrel as the mongrel among falcons, because of its unfalconly feeding habits including occasional piracy of bird nests and young. However, it has a special hunting method which all the other raptors except the blackwinged kite lack. It stops every now and then in flight and hovers in mid-air on rapidly beating wing tips, to scan the ground below for rodents, lizards, insects, etc. Spotting prey, it plummets silently to catch it in its talons before flying off to a safe perch.

Kaleej pheasant

Kaleej pheasant female

Monal pheasant pair

**Pheasants**

All pheasants of the world originated from the Himalaya and radiated into Tibet, China, Burma, Thailand, Vietnam, Indonesia, and the Caucasus mountains. Within India only the junglefowl and peafowl expanded their range to South India and Sri Lanka, long before man colonized the Indo-Gangetic plains. However, it is in its native home that this large family of beautiful birds has suffered the worst. Pressures from habitat destruction and deforestation in the Himalaya, combined with relentless hunting for meat and feathers, have put many species, including these monals (*Lophophorus sp.*) on the endangered list. The trade and hunting of all pheasants is now forbidden. Feathers and plumes of many pheasants, including the monal, and the *Kaleej* pheasant (*Lophura leucomelana*) are valued as decoration for headgear in several Himalayan cultures and their meat has been considered a delicacy. There is also a thriving trade in live birds.

Peacock

## Peafowl

India's National Bird, the peafowl (*Pavo cristatus*) is certainly one of the world's most beautiful birds. The cock bird displays a magnificent train that is actually not a tail but the extremely elongated feathers of the upper tail coverts, shed after the breeding season and regrown each year. But this heavy adornment does not handicap the bird flying between treetops or across ravines. Peafowl are birds of relatively dense scrub and deciduous forest in the vicinity of water and in their wild state, they are extremely alert and shy. Their alarm calls are among the first warnings to junglefolk of the presence of a predator or stranger. Closer to human habitation, their populations become quite tame and strut about in gardens, fallow fields and village streets. But wherever persecuted by poachers for meat or feathers, their paranoid behaviour and avoidance of human beings are a tell-tale sign of their plight.

Adult peacocks are polygamous, forming harems of up to six hens, and pompously display to them their fanned-out trains with much quivering and strutting. Peafowl in India have a diffuse breeding season from January to October, outside of which they generally live in all-male or all-female groups.

At night, peafowl roost on high tree branches and in arid areas telephone/electric poles serve the same purpose.

Peacock dancing

Grey partridge

### Partridges

One of our most popular game birds, the grey partridge (*Francolinus pondicerianus*) is a dumpy, greyish brown bird commonly seen in pairs or small groups in light forest and dry open country, and often in hedges of houses with large compounds. Partridge coveys spend large part of their time scraping the ground with their toes to seek out their food, which consists chiefly of grain, seeds, insect larvae, termites, etc. Cock birds are very pugnacious and use their spurs to engage in long fights with rival males. During courtship, males feed tid-bits to females. When surprised, this bird relies more on its feet than on flight for escape and runs quite fast to seek cover.

Chakor

### Chakor Partridge

In Indian fables there are numerous accounts of the chakor's love for the moon. In literature, the bird has always been connected with beauty and romance.

In its wild state the chakor (or chukor) partridge (*Alectoris graeca*) is distributed over Northern and Western Himalaya. It prefers rocky areas at reasonable altitudes and also lightly forested mountains. In winter, when food becomes scarce under a deep cover of snow, it migrates to lower altitudes. In Ladakh, however, their populations are resident in all the seasons.

Chakor are fighting birds and, if caught young, can be trained for fighting matches. They are fast fliers and provide good challenge to sportsmen.

Grey junglefowl

### Grey Junglefowl

In Central and South India the grey junglefowl (*Gallus sonneratii*) replaces its northern cousin, the red junglefowl (*Gallus gallus*). It lives in both light and dense forest and is extremely wary, though quite understandably, because it is among the favourite gamebirds for the table and is poached even in protected areas.

The best way to observe junglefowl is to sit up before dawn by a forest trail or a clearing, where small groups come out at first light to feed on insects, shoots, and grains.

Sarus cranes, courtship behaviour

### Sarus Cranes

Indian folklore is replete with tales of the love of the sarus couple towards each other, and of the pining away in grief by the bereaved partner. Indeed, the sarus crane (*Grus antigone*) is revered all over India as the symbol of marital fidelity, and popular sentiment protects it from being harmed. As a result, it lives quite confidently by the side of village ponds and on marshes near fields. It has occupied even railway-side ditches.

Sarus pair for life and the partners are nearly always seen together. They frequent riverbanks, cultivated fields, and bogs, where they feed on grains, juicy shoots, frogs, insects, and small reptiles. Sarus are the tallest flying birds of the world, reaching a height of 1.6 metres. They become very lovable and loyal pets, and make excellent sentinels for raising an alarm or actually assailing an intruder.

The nuptial ritual of a sarus pair, like all cranes, is one of the most unforgettable sights in Indian birdwatching. With wings outspread, both birds circle each other, bowing and dancing, frequently trumpeting in unison. Their nests are masses of reeds and other plant straws, built on slight mounds, usually in the middle of marshes or bogged fields, but sometimes even in fields away from water. Usually two eggs are laid and one or two chicks raised. The parents get quite pugnacious when guarding the eggs or young, and will furiously attack any intruding animal or person. Their egg shells are extraordinarily strong, which cannot be broken by crows or other thieving birds.

The sarus is resident over large parts of Northern, Central, and North-Eastern India. It is a unique example of how a bird species can co-exist with man, even surrounded by human activity, provided it has popular acceptance and its bare needs are met.

Blacknecked crane
incubating egg on nest

Blacknecked crane parents with chick

Blacknecked crane in its habitat. Ladakh.

### Blacknecked Crane

Of the world's 15 species of cranes, the blacknecked crane (*Grus nigricollis*) is the most endangered and the last one to be discovered. Also, it is the only crane that nests at high altitudes.

There are probably no more than 500 blacknecked cranes left worldwide. Within the Indian limits, fewer than 10 breeding pairs are known from Ladakh. Arunachal Pradesh, where a few pairs were reported till recent years, seems to have lost them. The Ladakh flock probably migrates to the lower altitudes of Tibet and a few birds may also be forming part of the wintering population in central and eastern Bhutan.

The blacknecked crane prefers marshy habitat around lakes or big rivers and builds its nest on a small elevated platform of mud or reeds, in the midst of marshy or waterlogged land. A pair may use the same nest site for years if left undisturbed. Both parents take turns at incubating the one or two eggs laid once a year. Inclement weather, including snowfall, is quite common during their incubation season, but the parents keep the eggs warm and dry, frequently turning them to ensure even development. Crane young are precocial and venture out of the nest soon after hatching. But because of sibling competition usually only one — the stronger chick — is raised to maturity. Perhaps this is Nature's way of ensuring that in an extremely hostile environment the scarce resources and the parents' energies are concentrated towards survival of only the hardiest progeny.

## Siberian Cranes

The breeding grounds of this rare crane (*Grus leucogeranus*) are in remote tundras by the Ob river in Siberia. There are two groups — a small western flock which winters in Iran and India, and the larger eastern flock which flies to Southern China.

International concern is building up as each successive winter fewer Siberian cranes arrive in the marshes of the Keoladeo Ghana National Park near Bharatpur, the only wintering habitat of this small group in India. Till only a hundred years ago these magnificent white birds used to winter in the rich wetlands over the entire Gangetic plains of North India. Over the past 15 years their numbers in India have fallen from about 80 to just 10 that came in the winter of 1990.

In Bharatpur they settle down amidst scores of other bird species in the shallow marshes, with their sub-adult chicks for whom this 6400-kilometre flight is their maiden migratory journey. While at Bharatpur they feed exclusively on the tubers of the sedge (*Cyperus rotundus*), which they dig out from the bottom mud. Staying here till March, they fly back to their breeding grounds.

Siberian cranes

Demoiselle crane

## Demoiselle Crane

The smallest member of the crane family, the demoiselle crane (*Anthropoides virgo*) is a distinctive looking bird, with ashy grey colouration and long, silky white tufts extending from behind each eye to the back of the neck. The neck is black with long, black, pointed feathers falling over the breast. The bird has a bright red iris.

Demoiselles are wanderers over the open plains and marshy lowlands, regularly visiting cultivated areas and sources of fresh water. In the Indian countryside they can be frequently seen raiding gram and wheat fields.

The local name for this crane — *koonj* — is onomatopoeic, deriving from the Sanskrit *kraunch*, the origin of the word 'crane' itself.

Coots

**Coots**

Among our commoner residents of the rail family, coots (*Fulica atra*) are easily identified by their ivory white frontal shields and pointed white bills. Their toes are typically long, and lobed along the sides.

The resident population is found throughout the summer, scattered over reedy tanks and ponds. With the arrival in winter of the migrant population from Central and West Asia, its numbers swell greatly. Their concentrations on lakes in winter form perhaps the largest bird congregations on water sheets in India. In their attempt to get airborne, coots first taxi rather comically on the water and flap vigorously until they have gained enough lift. But once they take off, they are strong fliers.

### Jacanas

Coloquially termed "lily trotters", jacanas are residents of the open water. They are unusually long-toed and leggy. These adaptations have enabled them to occupy the habitat offered by vegetation floating on the water's surface, as they can literally walk over water. The pheasant-tailed jacana (*Hydrophasianus chirurgus*) wears a long sickle shaped tail during the breeding season, a feature from which it derives its name. The bronze-winged jacana (*Metopidius indicus*) looks more like a moorhen, and is found closer to the swampy edges of a water body. Both birds lay their eggs on floating vegetation such as broad leaves, or sometimes between the tight tangles of rushes. The eggs, too are specially shaped, with one end conical and the other spherical, so that if the nest bobs on the water, they will roll back and forth in a tight circle and not fall into the water.

Both jacanas subsist on a mixture of aquatic vegetation and small animals such as insects and molluscs.

Brozewinged jacana

Pheasant-tailed jacana

### Indian Moorhen

Amphibious like its other cousins in the rail family, the Indian moorhen (*Gallinula chloropus*) is at home both on land and in the water. On the ground it skulks around on moist patches near water, foraging for insects, molluscs, or the seeds and shoots of marsh vegetation. The stubby tail is constantly flicked up to show the white patch on its underside. The bird is also extremely fond of swimming, and jerks its head to and fro with every paddling motion.

It is quite pugnacious and has a sharp call – emitted usually from hiding – which booms over the water. When alarmed, it rises low over the surface and escapes with rather laborious flight.

Indian moorhen with chicks

### White-breasted Waterhen

The white-breasted waterhen (*Amaurornis phoenicurus*) is a common sight by the edges of water bodies. It feeds on insects or vegetable matter, often boldly wandering some distance from cover, but bolts for safety at the slightest alarm. When foraging it keeps jerking up its short tail, to expose the rich red vent.

From its usual nature of quiet foraging, the bird sometimes takes to screeching and chuckling in a long drawn monotone; this behaviour becomes particularly obvious during the monsoon, its breeding season.

Whitebreasted waterhen

Great Indian bustards

Great Indian bustard

**Great Indian Bustard**
Excellent indicators of the health of their grassland and scrub-country habitat, bustards have declined in India over the past few decades. The combined pressures of hunting and habitat destruction once appeared to have all but wiped out our great Indian bustard (*Choriotis nigriceps*), a bird found nowhere else. Only strict protection in a few selected habitats has been able to revive their populations.

The great Indian bustard is commonly called 'hukna' because of its barking 'hook-hook' call. Standing up to four feet height, it reminds one of an ostrich. It has stout legs which aid it to run at good speeds. Its walk is stately and it flies only to escape. In western Rajasthan, where some of the best bustard habitats still remain, it associates with gazelle, fox, and jackal, among other animals. It is called 'godawan' here. It is extremely shy, cautious and wary when approaching the waterhole. Particularly vulnerable when drinking, it has to sit down on bent legs and after a sip it raises its neck to gulp water.

A male may have a single female, or a bevy of up to five. During the courtship display he puffs up a pouch in his neck, fluffing out the neck feathers and fanning up the tail. With wings drooped, the cock circles round his hens.

Oystercatcher

## Oystercatcher

Oystercatchers (*Haematopus ostralegus*) are conspicuous birds of the shores and estuaries where their food — shelled marine molluscs — is abundant. The bird has a stout red bill and pink legs that make it distinct. Oystercatchers are winter visitors to Indian coasts, but one population has been discovered breeding in the Sunderbans.

Venturing out at low tide, oystercatchers probe for worms and crabs in the wet sands. But their favourite food is the shelled molluscs such as clams, oysters, mussels, etc. The bird chisels with its bill into the bivalved shell and prises it open, to eat the flesh inside.

## Mongolian Plover

The lesser sand plover or Mongolian plover (*Charadrius mongolus*) breeds in Ladakh, migrating to the coastal regions of the Indian peninsula during the winter. It occurs in association with the great sand plover and is one of the commonest waders of our coastal areas. In its breeding plumage, during the summer in Ladakh, the bird has a striking black forehead and a rufous breast band.

Sand plovers are typically birds of shingle beaches, sandstrips along riverbanks and lake shores, and tidal mud flats. They run about in short spurts, stopping every now and then to jab down obliquely to pick up food, which comprises insects, larvae, and small molluscs. Although they forage in scattered parties, the entire flock gets up in flight together at the slightest alarm. It is a breathtaking sight to watch all the members of a flying plover flock twisting and turning in perfect synchronization.

Mongolian plover

**Redwattled Lapwing**

In India the ground plovers are collectively referred to as lapwings. Their most common representative here is the redwattled lapwing (*Vanellus indicus*), well known for its high pitched interrogating call 'Did you do it? Did you do it?', which gets highly neurotic at the slightest apprehension of intrusion during the nesting season. Its Hindi names, *Titehri* and *Huttitti*, are based on this call.

Lapwings prefer open country and scattered pairs can be seen around marshes, cultivation, and on pastures and wastelands. The bird runs in a characteristic plover fashion, going a short distance and then suddenly standing motionless. Its food comprises insects, worms, small molluscs, etc. It nests in a small depression on open ground, often using the dried and hardened pits of cattle hoofmarks around ponds.

The blotched eggs of a lapwing are perfectly camouflaged against the soil and are extremely difficult to find. If, however, either parent senses any danger to the eggs or the young, it performs what is called a 'broken wing' display to distract the intruder and lead it away from the nest. Sometimes it tries to mislead the intruder by a pseudo-incubation display — it sits down in a spot some distance away from its actual nest and pretends that it is incubating its eggs. When all else fails, both parents let loose an aerial assault, dive-bombing the intruder to the accompaniment of violent screaming. The chicks, too, are programmed by instinct to either freeze motionless or run and hide under vegetation, depending on the parents' commands and the emergency of the situation.

Redwattled lapwing

Redwattled lapwing in flight

Redshank

**Redshank**

An early morning birder scanning a lake or estuary can easily identify the redshank (*Tringa totanus*) by its repeated call of three trilling notes, 'triu hu hu', which carries long distances over the surface of water.

Redshanks are widely distributed over marshes, lakes, lagoons, and estuaries during the winter. They are usually found in mixed flocks consisting of several wader species. Our redshanks breed in Ladakh and Kashmir during the summer.

Blackwinged stilts

Blackwinged stilt (imm)

Avocet

**Blackwinged Stilts**

A long-legged, dainty wading bird with a white and grey, slender body and a long black bill, the blackwinged stilt (*Himantopus himantopus*) is a common sight at roadside ditches, shallow lagoons, seashores and other areas where water sheets develop even seasonally. Pairs or small groups wade into water to catch aquatic insects or probe for worms, etc. Groups can sometimes be seen swimming in deeper waters, thereby extending their range of activities far deeper than other waders of their size.

Quite placid within their own groups, they become agitated when disturbed by an intruder and the entire flock will then join forces to fight the outsider.

**Avocet**

The avocet (*Recurvirostra avosetta*) is a black and white marsh bird easily distinguished by its slender upcurved black bill and blue legs. It can be seen on tidal flats, marshes, lake shores, and lagoons, operating singly, or in pairs or small parties. It runs about in short spurts, and halts every now and then, holding its bill oblique to skim the water with the curved portion. It churns up the bottom mud with to and fro sweeping motions of the bill, and collects small prey organisms in its mandibles. It also feeds in open water by actively swimming with its webbed feet.

Avocets are mainly winter visitors to all of India's mainland. Within our territories, they breed in Kachchh, and maybe a few other localities.

**Stone Curlew**
**Greater Stone Plover**
Looking at their large, unblinking eyes, one can easily guess that stone curlews (*Burhinus oedicnemus*) are birds of the night. They are largely terrestrial and sedentary, and individuals keep to the same localities. Stone curlews are partial to the deciduous zone, within which they inhabit rocky hills and mounds, dry lakebeds and river tracts, light scrub, village groves, and wooded gardens in cities.

They spend the daytime standing, resting on bent legs, or squatting, in some inaccessible thicket amidst groves or shrubbery, and do not move at all until threatened by an animal or very nearly trodden upon. Even when flushed out of their hiding, they prefer to run or fly a short distance, and they suddenly crouch and freeze, to totally merge into their stony surroundings, thanks to the perfect camouflage provided by their plumage. At dusk they become active and emerge to feed on worms, insects, and small reptiles.

Stone curlew

Greater stone plover

Brownheaded gull

**Gulls**

These gulls were photographed in their breeding colonies in Ladakh, where they nest in the summer. Most species of gulls are in a different plumage or colour phase when they are in their non-breeding, or wintering, quarters. To add to the birdwatcher's miseries, first and second year immatures of almost all the gulls are confusingly similar.

In Ladakh, the gulls scoop fish from the surface waters and probably catch other aquatic animals also, from the edge of the water. In their wintering areas – both the eastern and western coasts and several inland water bodies – they supplement their food by pirating fish from fishing villages and boats, or by scrounging for castaway scraps. Here they compete with the resident kites, crows and other species of gulls. They are reported to sometimes catch insects and, surprisingly, eat juicy shoots of crops.

Blackheaded gulls (imm)

Great blackheaded gull

A solitary bird, the great blackheaded gull (*Larus ichthyaetus*) is easily identifiable, being the largest of the Indian gulls. In its summer plumage the adult bird has black head and neck, and slaty grey body. There are two small white patches, one circling the eye above and the other below. The yellow bill has a red tip.

In winter, this gull is a visitor to the Indian coasts. Its summer distribution in India has not been reported, but I have photographed and observed this bird in the Zanskar valley, Ladakh, in summer.

Among the gulls that breed in the high-altitude region of Ladakh is also the black-headed gull *(L.ichthyaetus)*.

Snow pigeons

Blue rock pigeon

**Blue Rock Pigeon**

The cosmopolitan family of pigeons, doves, and sandgrouses has a large number of representative species in India. Its commonest example, the blue rock pigeon (*Columba livia*), has a worldwide distribution. As its name suggests, it is originally a bird of rocky and cliff habitat. All domestic strains have been selectively and artificially bred from this wild ancestor. It is still found in such wild state, but those near habitation have become commensals of man, totally adapted to living in noisy, congested surroundings, and proliferating as a result of popular acceptance. In many big cities their huge populations have assumed pest proportions.

Rock pigeons are mainly granivorous and in the wild their flocks settle in freshly seeded fields, fallow lands, and open cultivation to feed on seeds and grains. In cities they are dependent on man for their food, picking up grain and scraps of food from households, pavements, railway platforms, and grain holdings such as godowns and silos. Several cities have their own 'Trafalgar Squares' — extremely popular spots where bird lovers and the devout scatter grains for the pigeon throngs that collect there, or handfeed the birds.

**Snow Pigeon**

Closely related to the Turkestan pigeon and similar in its habitat preferences, the snow pigeon (*Columba leuconota*) is a brown and white bird, identified in overhead flight by its white body and blackish head. Snow pigeons in the Himalaya range from 3000 m to 5000 m elevations during the summer, coming down to lower altitudes in winter. They roost on cliffs or in trees. Pairs or small flocks are commoner in summer. They visit mountain villages and feed on freshly sown grain crops in the fields. Otherwise they flock on the boulders or on grassy meadows and glean seeds from grasses and weeds.

Rufous dove

Turkman pigeons

**Turkman Pigeons**
The Turkestan or Turkman pigeon (*Columba rupestris turkestanica*) is widely found all over Ladakh, Kashmir, Lahul and Spiti. Similar to the common rock pigeon in habits and breeding, it can be distinguished by the broad white band on its back and tail. When a flock in flight wheels, there is a sudden flash of white, the sight of which is an unforgettable experience for anyone.

Turkman pigeons live in colonies on rocky cliffs and precipitous gorges, nesting among the hundreds of ledges and other niches in such habitats. Large flocks visit villages and cultivation to feed on grain and seeds. They also regularly visit high mountain passes where devotees scatter grain.

Spotted dove

Doves
The pigeon family in India has several species of doves. Among the most beautiful of them is the spotted dove (*Streptopelia chinensis*), unmistakable because of its striking spotted patterns on the back and the 'chessboard' markings at the base of the hindneck. It is a resident of the better wooded areas and tends to prefer lush tracts, avoiding dry habitats.

This and the other species of doves are chiefly grain eaters. They flock around in fields to pick seeds and grains from fresh sowings, or visit village roads where grain carts usually drop some grain during loading and transport. If not harmed, they become quite tame and confiding, as in our villages, and will freely enter households to eat the grain scattered during winnowing work in homes, or put out by the religious and the devout. Doves have calls that range from pleasant to harsh, but their song has traditionally been considered mournful. Like pigeons, dove pairs also like sitting close together, which explains the expression 'lovey dovey'!

Blossom-headed parakeet female

**Parakeets**
Of all the Indian birds that have the capability to copy human vocabulary, the roseringed parakeet (*Psittacula krameri*) is second only to the hill myna. For this, as also for its ability to learn a few performing tricks, it is at the centre of a huge trade in cagebirds. Countless numbers of young are removed from their nests by trappers, for sale as pets. Only the male has the rose-coloured ring around its neck. The blossomheaded parakeet (*Psittacula cyanocephala*), a closely related bird of generally similar habits, is a denizen of relatively better wooded areas and keeps to forests or groves around cultivation. Its bluish red head (slaty grey in females) and the questioning, musical call (tooi?) make it easily identifiable. It is the swiftest flier among all the parakeets and displays a variety of twists and turns while a flock flies through a forest. The largest of this group, the Alexandrine parakeet (*Psittacula eupatria*) is similar to the roseringed parakeet, but its larger size and the presence of a maroon patch on each shoulder sets it apart from the others. The female lacks the ring around the neck.

Parakeets are familiar, noisy birds seen in orchards, woodlands, city parks and gardens, cultivation, etc. Large flocks often attain pest status as they cause heavy damage to fruit crops and other cultivation. In their wasteful style, they drop, or damage by gnawing, more than they eat, inviting the farmer's wrath.

Rose-ringed parakeet male

Blossom-headed parakeet male

Alexandrime or Large Indian parakeet female

Parakeet courtship is a joy to watch. The male brings offerings of food to the female, and uses comical head and foot movements accompanied by sweet beckoning calls for communication. The pair engage in prolonged 'kissing' by locking beaks or snuggle up cosily in between short spells of mating. Their nests are made in tree hollows, either natural or excavated. Parakeets may even nest on an inaccessible cranny in a vertical rockface or a wall. Both parents take part in rearing the chicks. Apart from their sharp toes, they also use their beaks for climbing and employ their long tails, pressed hard against vertical surfaces, for retaining balance.

### Cuckoos

Cuckoos are harbingers of the monsoon over North and West India. Silent and unnoticed throughout the winter, they become suddenly active and noisy as the hot weather advances, chasing one another through gardens and fighting resident crows and babblers. Their calls, too, by which these birds are best known, reach a peak just before the onset of the monsoon.

The cuckoo family has several specialists in nest parasitism. Koel (*Eudynamys scolopacea*), hawk cuckoo (*Cuculus varius*), and pied crested cuckoo (*Clamator jacobinus*) are some of the birds who do not make their own nests. Instead, the female sneaks up to an unguarded nest of another bird that is incubating its eggs and lays an egg in it, after removing one egg from the nest. The cuckoo egg is the first to hatch and the chick sees to the job of throwing out the legitimate eggs or any chicks that hatch. The foster parents faithfully feed and rear the cuckoo, which soon outgrows them. It matures in about 3-4 weeks and leaves the nest.

Pied-crested cuckoo

Black cuckoo

Koel

Spotted owlet

Great horned owl

**Owls**

Owls are a good example of how a bird can suffer more on account of superstition than from habitat destruction or any other reason. Described in mythology as *Brahma's* carrier, in real life an owl is not too welcome a bird in most Indian societies except in Bengal, where it is worshipped as a bird of good omen. Their beneficial role in controlling rodent populations notwithstanding, people try to rid the neighbourhood of owls by stoning the bird and breaking their nests.

Owls have a wide repertoire of sounds which include hoots, screeches, whistles, screams shrieks, chatters, laughs and growls. In addition, they also click their beaks and clap their wings to produce sounds.

The spotted owlet (*Athene brama*) is widespread over India's habitats, except dense forest. It occupies hollow tree trunks, abandoned nest holes in trees and ruins and, if tolerated, takes up residence in crevices in the walls or ceilings of houses. Usually inactive by day, it flies out at dusk to catch mice, lizards, insects and unguarded bird babies. At night, entire families can be seen on roads passing through wilderness, feasting on insects swarming around the lamp posts and frogs and lizards killed by vehicles. Owls have large eyes, adapted to night vision which is 100 times more acute than human eyes, and their flight on rounded wings is extremely silent. In pitch dark, owls depend more on their acute sense of hearing than on sight for prey location.

**Nightjar**
The Indian jungle nightjar (*Caprimulgus indicus*) is resident over practically all of India, south of the Himalaya. It is a bird of open scrub and deciduous forest, both in the plains and in the hills up to about 2300 m elevations.

Nightjars are purely crepuscular and nocturnal. All day long they hide in the shade of dense tree foliage, perfectly camouflaged by their cryptic colouration and their strange habit of sitting along the length of the branch, unlike other birds, who sit across. Sometimes one may surprise them from their roosting spots amidst vegetation or stones on the ground. The monotonous, prolonged *chuckoo chuckoo chuckoo chuckoo* .... calls of nightjars, which commence at dusk, are among the most familiar sounds of the Indian jungle by night.

Nightjars are insectivorous birds and start their feeding activity soon after dusk, when they emerge from their roosts to chase and catch flying insects such as moths, bugs, termites, and beetles. They are often found sitting on roads at night, and brilliant ruby red light is reflected by their eyes from the beams of vehicle headlights.

**House Swift (*Apus affinis*)**
Swifts are birds of unusual qualities. They spend most part of the day flying almost non-stop. Their beaks can open disproportionately wide to aid the capture of winged insect prey in rapid flight. They cannot perch ordinarily like other birds, since all four toes in their feet are forwardly directed. So they cling to the rough surfaces of cliffs, buildings, and old, ruined structures such as forts. They cement their cup-shaped nests of feather and straw with their own saliva, to ceilings, walls, the undersides of eaves and arches in buildings, often right inside occupied dwellings.

Nightjar

House swift

Pied kingfisher

Whitebreasted kingfisher

Little blue kingfisher

### Kingfishers

Kingfishers are specialists in the art of catching fish from the surface waters. Each species has its unique method. The whitebreasted kingfisher (*Halcyon smyrnensis*) sits patiently at its favourite perch — an overhanging branch, a post or an overhead wire — overlooking water and scans the surface. On noticing the movement of its potential prey, it flies low over the water and catches the fish in its bill. Back at the perch, it batters the victim to death and swallows it whole. Though it is chiefly a fish eater, the whitebreasted kingfisher frequently eats lizards, grasshoppers, and rarely mice, which it catches by pouncing from a vantage post.

Its cousin, the pied kingfisher (*Ceryle rudis*) has perfected quite another method. It can hover in mid-air over the same spot for several minutes at a stretch. It thus scans the water underneath and plummets down to grab fish, frog or tadpole from near the surface, to carry it away to its perch and swallow it after battering the victim. This species is more associated with water bodies such as *jheels*, rivers, ditches and tidal creeks, as compared with the former, which can be encountered quite some distance away from water, in forest patches and lightly wooded areas.

Blue jay

## Small Green Bee-eater

As its name suggests, this dainty little bird (*Merops orientalis*) specializes in preying upon winged insects, particularly bees, wasps, termites, dragonflies, winged ants, butterflies, and moths. From its favourite perch on a branch, an overhead cable or a fencepost, it sorties behind passing prey and catches it in mid-air. It then flies back to its perch, where it beats the victim against a hard surface before swallowing it.

Bee-eaters commonly go about in loose flocks or hunting parties. They sleep lazily till late in the morning and then start their feeding activity, which continues into the afternoon. At dusk the entire rabble will settle noisily in a leafy tree to roost for the night, amidst occasional squabbles for preferred perching spots.

Green Bee-eater

Blue jay

## Blue Jay

The Indian roller or blue jay (*Coracias benghalensis*) is a rather big-headed bird, easily recognized by its striking turquoise blue colours in wings, brown breast, and blue abdomen. The various hues of blue appear as brilliant flashes in flight.

Blue jays can be commonly seen perched on overhead wires, fence posts or on steep earthbanks or mounds, and are among the most familiar birds seen during a train journey in the Indian countryside. Scanning the surroundings from its perch, a roller flies down to capture a large insect or a frog or a lizard, then flies off to a perch where it stuns the victim to death before proceeding to eat it. When at rest, it usually keeps moving its tail up and down in slow motion.

Several birds, rollers included, display a fascinating form of behaviour termed as anting. Occasionally a bird will squat flat on its belly on some ant-ridden spot, and press its outspread wings to the ground. It is believed that these birds do so to induce the ants to sting them, because the formic acid the birds so receive in their skins and feathers is a strong antiseptic, keeping their plumage clean and free of infection.

Hoopoe

## Hoopoe

A very familiar bird of gardens and lawns, the hoopoe (*Upupa epops*) is conspicuously patterned and coloured. It also occurs in open country and light forest. The bird has an erectile crest which it fans out when it is excited or uneasy, or when alighting.

Hoopoes are completely insectivorous. They move about on the ground, probing the debris and digging with their curved beaks for insects such as crickets, locusts, earwigs, beetles, etc. and their larvae. Its call, a two or three note 'hoo po, hoo po po' gave the bird its common name.

Great Indian hornbill

## Great Indian Hornbill

*Buceros bicornis*, a handsome dweller of evergreen and moist deciduous forests has suffered extensively due to the destruction and degradation of its forest habitats. It is a fruit eater and nearly completely arboreal, only very occasionally coming down to the ground to pick up fallen berries or other fruit. The prominent helmet is hollow and very light. Its function is not known.

Hornbills are very partial to fruiting trees, particularly banyan, peepul and other figs. Here they congregate in noisy feeding groups, constantly communicating with one another in a rich vocabulary that comprises various grunts, roars, and barks.

Hornbills have a most fascinating nesting behaviour. They use natural hollows high up in some giant trees as nest holes and the female traps herself in by 'walling in' the entrance hole with a mixture of her excreta, mud brought in by the male and crushed vegetable matter such as pulp. The wall dries into a hard barrier and only a narrow slit is left, through which the male hands in food for the female, and later for the family. The female and the young eject their excreta through this hole with force. When the chicks are a little grown, the wall is broken to allow the mother to come out and join the father in foraging but the nest is re-walled. When the chicks are old enough to leave the nest, the parents break the wall.

Coppersmiths mating

**Coppersmith**

Anyone trying to locate this bird by its loud and ringing call will know how frustrating such search can be, because the crimson-breasted barbet (*Megalaima haemacephala*) is a gifted ventriloquist. Hidden in the topmost branches, it spends long hours monotonously uttering its 'tuk-tuk' call, reminiscent of a coppersmith hammering metal, which gives the bird its name.

Barbets prefer wooded areas and are partial to fruiting trees, particularly those with figs or berries, which form their staple diet. When swarms of winged termites emerge, they sometimes hawk these insects in mid-air.

Offering food to the female is an interesting part of the male's courtship behaviour in several bird families, including the barbets. They nest in tree hollows excavated in the boles of softwood species such as coral (*Erythrina*) or kachnar (*Bauhinia*), usually in the scars left by dead and fallen branches. Sometimes they also occupy the abandoned nest holes of woodpeckers.

Coppersmith male feeding female

Green barbet

**Green Barbet**

The green barbet (*Megalaima zeylanica*) is common throughout the wooded areas, gardens, and groves of the Indian plains and lower hills. Its overall green plumage provides it excellent camouflage in its arboreal hideouts. It also has a prolonged repetitive call 'Kuturr-kuttur', and 'Kutok-kutok'.

### Goldenbacked Woodpecker

The commonest of India's woodpeckers, *Dinopium benghalense* can be found in any wooded area throughout the country. Its flashy colours stand out against tree trunks; the dipping flight is diagnostic, visible even from a distance, and its alarm call during flight is like loud cackling laughter. The female lacks the red crest.

Woodpeckers derive their family name from their habit of tapping and chiselling tree bark or logs of wood, to get at their food — termites, beetles, grubs, and other insect parasites of wood — from under the surface. They tap their way up trees either straight or in spirals round the bole, occasionally going backwards for short spurts.

They enlarge hollows in tree stems or branches to use as nests and both parents participate in all domestic duties.

Goldenbacked woodpecker

### Larks

Larks are a widespread family of ground-nesting birds. The small skylark (*Alauda gulgula*) is found throughout India in open country and grassland. Of all the larks it is perhaps the best known for its lively performance of fluttering up vertically and delivering a sustained, chirruping song. The other species, the horned lark (*Eremophila alpestris*) lives in the cold-desert regions of North-western Himalaya. It has two 'horns' (tufts of long narrow feathers) on either side of its head. This lark probably migrates altitudinally according to season, but in general it prefers stony habitat with scant vegetation. It is a common bird of the high Himalayan habitats, and appears in large flocks during its non-breeding phase. It is bold and confiding, and allows close approach, even when nesting. It is commonly seen in the vicinity of mountain encampments, and frequently picks up the stray floss from sheep wool to line its nest.

Both the larks are chiefly seed eaters, but supplement their diet with insects.

Horned lark male

Horned lark female on nest. Ladakh.

Small skylark

Wiretailed swallows

**Wiretailed Swallow**
Deriving its name from the two long 'wires' that develop in its tail during each breeding cycle, the wiretailed swallow (*Hirundo smithii*) is always found in association with water. Unlike the other swallows, it does not form large swarms and the only social group is a number of birds sharing the same tree or power line as a perch, or several pairs nesting under the same rock overhang or bridge, though not constituting a colony even at this stage. Swallows hawk for flying insects, keeping their mouth open in flight, even scooping water from pools and streams in the same manner.

Baybacked shrike

### Shrikes

Popularly referred to as the butcherbirds, shrikes are a family of predatory birds that live on insects, small reptiles, rodents, and frogs. They often kill even when they do not require to, and then store the prey by impaling it on thorns, sharp stumps, and the spikes of fenceposts and barbed wire fencing.

The baybacked shrike (*Lanius vittatus*) shown here is a gifted mimic and quickly learns to copy several calls and sounds.

Grey shrike

Golden oriole male

Golden oriole female feeding chicks

Golden oriole chick

**Golden Oriole**

Despite its flashy colours, the golden oriole (*Oriolus oriolus*) camouflages itself effectively in the upper foliage of dense trees where it spends a large part of the day, eating figs, berries and other fruits or hunting insects. The bird is partial to trees of the fig family as also to fruit groves. Its loud melodious whistling calls ('peelooloo peelooloo') usually indicate its presence and with patience a brief glimpse may be the reward. Their hammock shaped nests are distinct and prove helpful in locating the birds.

The male has black in its plumage contrasting vividly with its golden yellow colour and bright red eyes, whereas the female is uniform ovive green colour.

Orioles are extremely shy of human presence and fly away from their nests at the slightest suspicion. But they remain in the vicinity and maintain a close vigil from cover, returning immediately to fight any predator or nest raider, such as a crow approaching the eggs or young.

Common myna

Mynas

Brahminy myna

rahminy myna

Pied myna

Bank myna

**Mynas**

The common myna (*Acridotheres tristis*) is one of the most familiar commensals of man and is found in the vicinity of human habitations all over the country. It can be seen running alongside tractors in the fields or strutting about in busy streets, on city lawns, and merrily intruding into households to pick up scraps of food or insects.

A tuft of hair dangling from the back of the adult bird's head, reminiscent of a Brahmin's *'choti'* gives *Sturnus pagodarum* its common name — Brahminy myna. Its close cousin, the pied myna (*Sturnus contra*) gets its name from the pie-shaped white patch on its cheek. Both these mynas are largely ground birds, although both nest in trees. They are omnivorous, scrounging for scraps among refuse dumps, searching out seeds from cattle dung, attending on grazing cattle to catch insects disturbed by their movements through pastures, and eat berries, figs, and flower parts of several trees. Both birds are impulsive chatterers and have an impressive repertoire of notes.

The brahminy myna nests in hollows of tree boles or ruins, while the pied myna builds a huge, shaggy nest of plant material and rubbish, quite often with a bright red or blue rag in it. The nest has a globular roof and a single entrance on one side.

Apparently vicious fights frequently erupt among myna groups, with a great deal of screaming, beating and pinning one another down. But these are harmless jousts and mynas seem to enjoy them, taking just any opportunity to engage in such bouts. They are inveterate nest raiders.

Tree pie

**Tree Pie**

The Indian tree pie (*Dendrocitta vagabunda*) is an extremely bold and inquisitive bird, like the crow. In many forest habitats, in fact, it is the ecological equivalent of the common crow. It is found in scrub jungle and gardens throughout the plains and foothills.

In sanctuaries with regular human presence, tree pies have taken to raiding camps and kitchens to pick up scraps of food. Individual birds are even trained to feed off people's hands. Tree pies are truly omnivorous, eating human foods, fruits, berries, insects, lizards, rodents, young birds and bats, frogs, and even carrion. It is a noisy bird with a range of harsh calls, but also has a musical whistling note.

**Whitecheeked Bulbul**

This is a cheerful bulbul found all over North and North-West India, in lightly wooded areas and gardens in towns and villages. In the wild it feeds on berries, insects and nectar, but around habitations, especially in rural India, it is quite bold and confiding, entering houses to pick up scraps of food. It is not at all shy of humans and will allow very close approach.

It is extremely interesting to watch a pair sitting close and cocking their heads and chattering as if passing sarcastic comments on their human neighbours.

The race shown here is the northern *Pycnonotus leucogenys leucogenys*, ranging over the Himalayan states and North-Western areas.

Whitecheeked bulbul

**Redvented Bulbul**

One of our most familiar and melodious birds, the redvented bulbul (*Pycnonotus cafer*) is found throughout the sub-continent upto heights of 4000 feet, above which the black bulbul more or less replaces it.

It is mainly arboreal in habits and large numbers collect on trees or shrubs that have juicy fruit or berries, such as the fig family and, surprisingly, Lantana. It also catches termites when swarms emerge in their winged phase. Bulbuls in cities and villages frequently learn to accept food handed out to them, just like sparrows.

Redvented bulbul

Jungle babbler

**Babblers**
A very common bird of the plains and foothills, the jungle babbler (*Turdoides striatus*) is usually seen in flocks of more than half a dozen, thus earning its various colloquial names — seven sisters, *sat bhai*, and *sat saheli*. Noisy birds, their flocks are always blabbering among themselves and loud quarrels frequently stir up over trivia. But the flock shows up united when there is danger in the form of a predator or an intruder.

Babblers are not too discerning in their food preferences and rummage through ground debris for scraps of food, insects, spiders, fallen berries and seeds, occasionally eating nectar from flowers of coral and silk cotton.

Babblers are communal nesters. Several females lay in a common nest and then share all the nest guarding and domestic duties. This behaviour seems to have emerged from the bird's discovery of the security and economy in jointly sharing these duties.

Ashy wren warbler

**Ashy Wren Warbler**
Warblers constitute a large family of extremely confusing bird species. Perhaps the commonest of the wren warblers in North India, the ashy wren warbler (*Prinia socialis*) is a fidgety little bird seen flitting from bush to bush in scrub country, open grounds, hedgerows or gardens. It also occurs in light deciduous forest, and is a resident in nearly all parts of the plains and hills up to about 2000 m.

The bird is quite bold and enters households and gardens to catch its insect diet. It fearlessly nests in domestic hedges. The nest is usually a basket-shaped structure of fibres, suspended low amidst shrubbery, but sometimes stitched leaf nests — like those of tailor birds — may also be found.

### Magpie-Robin

Rather unnoticed for the rest of the year, the magpie-robin (*Copsychus saularis*) turns into an accomplished melodist with the onset of its breeding season early in the summer. Males can then be seen singing and displaying from their perches, with repeated jerking up of the tail in a robin style.

Silk-cotton and coral trees in flower are favourite sites for magpie-robins, which they visit to sip nectar. Their staple diet is insects, which they pick while hopping about in the undergrowth.

Magpie robin

Alpine accentor

Robin accentor

Robin accentor nest and chicks

### Accentors

The accentors are closely related to chats and thrushes. In India, all 8 species of this family are denizens of the Himalaya, 6 of these breeding at extremely high altitudes. The Alpine accentor (*Prunella collaris*) and the Robin accentor (*Prunella rubeculoides*) are close cousins.

They are unobtrusive birds, hopping about on the ground, occasionally displaying wing-flicking behaviour. Around their breeding season (June-July) these birds generally keep in pairs. Later in the summer they can be seen in small flocks, which swell up to 20-25 birds by September.

Magpie robin brown-backed race

### Whitebreasted Dipper

The dipper family has a unique specialization, it occupies a niche in nature no other bird group has been able to adapt to – the rapid mountain streams and torrents – and lives exclusively on the insect life in such icy cold waters. It makes its nests in or under an overhanging bush on the stream bank and the entrance to the nest is via underwater approach.

The one shown here is an immature whitebreasted dipper (*Cinclus cinclus cashmeriensis*), a resident of the Himalayan mountains. It is a territorial bird and individuals or parties are found separated by large stretches of stream and boulder habitat. It feeds by darting into the stream from its rock perches and swimming strongly against the current, taking help from its legs to find the bottom, thus actually 'walking' against the stream flow. It can remain submerged for considerable periods and catches insects or larvae from the water. Periodically it emerges from the water to shake itself dry and take a short break before plunging in again.

Whitebreasted dipper chick or imm

Guldenstadt's redstart

Black redstart

### Redstart

One of the hardiest Indian thrushes, Guldenstadt's redstart (*Phoenicurus erythrogaster grandis*) is a resident of some of the most inhospitable Himalayan terrain and harsh climate. Within the Indian limits, its range extends from Ladakh to Kumaon, and to Sikkim and Arunachal Pradesh. Its breeding has been recorded from elevations as high as 5500 m in Tibet, and its wintering range extends from 1500 m to 4800 m. The bird prefers scrub thickets, boulders and rocky hillsides, usually close to streams.

It is an extremely shy bird, difficult to observe for any length of time. In behaviour it is a typical redstart, flitting from boulder to boulder, occasionally flying down to pick an insect from the ground. It also chases and catches insects in flight.

Large pied wagtail

## White Wagtail

Of the three races of white wagtail (*Motacilla alba*) that are found wintering over most of India, only one, masked white wagtail (*M.a. personata*), breeds within India, in Ladakh and Kashmir. From May to July, its nests can be found tucked away in stone piles or in holes in old walls.

At the onset of winter, these birds fly down to spread over the Indian plains and peninsula, where they add to the large number of migrants of the other two races (*dukhunensis* and *occularis*) from North Asia and Siberia. Mixed flocks can then be seen running about on open grasslands, gardens and fields, wagging their tails up and down. They feed on small insects picked up from the ground.

Another wagtail that breeds in the Kashmir Himalaya is the yellowheaded wagtail (*Motacilla citreola*). In winter large flocks arrive in the plains of North and Central India where they settle on marshy tracts and grassy waterfronts. Displaying behaviour typical of the wagtail family these birds sometimes chase insects in flight or on floating lily leaves.

## Yellow Wagtail

Shown here is the winter phase of the yellow wagtail (*Motacilla flava*), a winter visitor to India. The three races — blueheaded, greyheaded and blackheaded — are difficult to tell apart during this phase.

While with us in the plains, these birds prefer marshy grounds or lush fields where they catch insects, flitting about in short spurts, incessantly wagging their tails up and down (hence the name). They form into huge flocks to fly to and from their roosts, usually amidst dense reedbeds or rushes. Ladakh forms the southern part of their breeding range.

Yellow wagtail

Wagtail nest and chicks

## Purple Sunbird

Like their close relatives, hummingbirds, the sunbirds (*Nectarinia asiatica*) are nectar feeders. Their needle sharp, curved bills and tubular tongues are perfect examples of evolution for a nectarine existence. These aid the birds to probe deep down into flowers and suck the nectar. They supplement this diet with occasional catches of insects and spiders. These adaptations also enable them to suck water dripping from wet objects, for example dew drops from moss, as this female is doing here. Breeding males attain a brilliant, glossy plumage. They also indulge in a spirited display before the females, which involves singing from high perches and drooping of the wings.

Yellowheaded wagtail

## White-Eye

White-eyes (*Zosterops palpebrosa*) get their name from the prominent white rings around their eyes. They are common birds of gardens and wooded areas, resident over the entire country except the extremely arid parts.

White-eyes are entirely arboreal. Single birds or small flocks go about flower beds and trees with juicy fruits. They live largely on nectar and fruit pulp, but also catch insects from crevices.

White-eye

Masked white wagtail

Yellowthroated sparrow

Sunbird female

## Yellowthroated Sparrow

Identifiable by its overall sparrow looks and a yellow throat patch, the yellowthroated sparrow (*Petronia xanthocollis*) is more a bird of scrub jungle, and even when found in towns and other habitations it is not so closely linked to man as the house sparrow. In its scrub habitat it feeds on insects, nectar, and wild berries. Where it lives in the vicinity of cultivation, flocks may form to pick seeds and grains from fields. It has a number of chirpy calls so similar to the house sparrow's but more musical. They form mixed flocks with munias and are best observed at waterholes and surrounding trees in arid zones.

Streaked weaver bird female

Streaked weaver bird

**Streaked Weaver Bird**
In their non-breeding phase the weaver birds are difficult to distinguish from sparrows. But with the onset of the breeding season, the male attains his flamboyant black and yellow plumage, like this streaked weaver bird (*Ploceus manyar*) male, when parties of males hectic nest-building activity. Using the green skin of reeds, rice straw, grass and other fine twigs, each male weaves several hanging flask-shaped nests, suspended from branches of trees usually overhanging water. When the nests are half done, groups of drab females visit the colony to inspect them, while the males go into frenzied displays, quivering and drooping their wings and chirping to attract a potential mate. If a female approves of a male's nest, she expresses it by settling down. The male then finishes the nest, adding an entry tunnel, which is the crucial part of the nest since it makes the structure virtually predator-proof. The vertical tunnel opens from beneath and none but weaver birds know how to fly straight up into it. This technique of vertical entry offers effective protection against nest-raiding birds and snakes.

Weaver bird males are polygamous and have several nests with a female each at the same time. Some males fail to attract a female till the end of the laying period; they leave their nests unfinished in despair.

## Munias

Resident in almost all the arid tracts of India and occurring up to 6,000 feet high in the Himalaya, the whitethroated munia (*Lonchura malabarica*) is partial to dry open country with scanty scrub, as also open cultivation. Its close cousin, the spotted munia (*Lonchura punctulata*) is also found almost all over India but avoids the dry regions of Punjab, Haryana and Rajasthan. The munia family is largely granivorous, only occasionally catching winged termites during the latter's swarming phase.

Munias go about in haphazard flocks consisting of family groups and their flight is typically undulating. If undisturbed, they settle in a patch of reeds or grass in seed, or in a crop field, to eat the grains from the plants or the ground. In the quiet of the countryside a birdwatcher can easily locate such a flock by the sounds of cracking plant stems and grains and the intermittent, feeble chirping of the birds. But when alarmed the whole flock rises with a whir to either fly away or dart into the shelter of the nearest trees.

Nesting goes on all year round, with local variations in intensity. Munias build large, round nests of rough grasses and strips of skin peeled from ripening crop stems. They line the insides with cotton wool and soft grass. Roosting flocks frequently use abandoned nests as shelter.

Spotted munias

White-throated munia

Greenfinch

## Great Rosefinch

Great rosefinch (*Carpodacus rubicilla severtzovi*) is quite common in the high Himalayan habitats, but within its wide range in the Indian subcontinent – Ladakh, Sikkim, Lahul and Spiti — it is found patchily distributed over small, separate localities. In the summer in Ladakh, it is seen in bouldery habitat at the base of mountains, and regularly visits villages and neighbouring fields. Its food consists chiefly of berries and seeds and also some insects. They are frequent feeders at the cook houses of Army outposts.

Great rosefinch

## Himalayan Greenfinch

Finches are seed eaters, as their short beaks would indicate. Greenfinches eat seeds of many kinds, including sunflower, millets, rice, hemp, and many other crops that may vary with locality. They also take berries and insects.

The Himalayan greenfinch (*Carduelis spinoides*) breed in summer in the Himalaya, at elevations between 2000 and 4400 m. They spend the winters lower down in the foothills, below 1500 m. The are partial to open slopes, forest edges, and cultivation.

Crested bunting

# Bibliography


Ali, Salim: *The Book of Indian Birds.* First published in 1941. Revised and expanded edition 1972. A popular handbook. Bombay Natural History Society (BNHS).

Ali, Salim & S. Dillon Ripley: *Handbook of the Birds of India and Pakistan,* 10 vols., An encyclopaedic study. BNHS.

Baker, E.C. Stuart: *Fauna of British India—Birds,* 8 vols. 1922-30. Ample plumage descriptions, though considered obsolete on scientific data.

Jerdon, T.C.: *The Birds of India,* 3 vols., 1862-64. Detailed information on habits. The first thorough-going study, by a leading authority of the last century. Eminently readable.

Oates, E.W. & W.T. Blanford: *Fauna of British India—Birds,* 4 vols., 1889-98. The bird volumes are part of a study of Indian natural history. The line drawings are mostly of heads.

Ripley, S. Dillon: *A Synopsis of the Birds of India and Pakistan,* 1961. A copious reference guide, details range and status; preceded the *Handbook.*

Whistler, Hugh: *The Popular Handbook of Indian Birds,* 1949. Worthwhile, but not a comprehensive guide, written by a brilliant field ornithologist.

**Guides & textbooks on the birds of neighbouring areas**

Etchecopar, R.D. & F. Hue: *Les Oiseaux de Chine, de Mongolie et de Coree,* 2 vols. (in French), 1978-83. An extensive reference book.

Hartet, E.: *Die Vogel der Palaarktischen Fauna,* 3 vols. and supplement (in German), 1903-38. Encyclopaedic descriptions of the birds of the Palearctic region, which touches the Himalayas.

Hue, F. & R.D. Etchecopar: *Les Oiseaux du Proche et du Moyen Orient,* 1970 (in French). A Guide to the birds of the Middle East.

King, B.M.W. Woodcock & E.C. Dickenson: *A Field Guide to the Birds of South-East Asia.* A detailed, illustrated, handbook. Refers to several birds occurring in the Himalaya and India.

Oates, E.W.: *A Handbook to the Birds of British Burma,* 2 vols., 1883.

Paludan, K.: *On the Birds of Afghanistan,* 1959.

Smythies, B.E.: *The Birds of Burma,* 1953. A thorough reference book.

Vaurie, C: *The Birds of the Palearctic Fauna,* 2 vols., 1959-65. An important taxonomic study. Many species referred to, breed in the Himalaya or winter in India.

*Tibet and its Birds,* 1972. A good introduction to the birds of this region.

**General Reading**

A list of important titles on natural history, travel and background reading which would be valuable for understanding the fascinating flora and wildlife of an exciting setting for bird-life.

Adams, A.L.: *Wanderings of a Naturalist in India,* 1867. Written by a much-travelled and observant army surgeon, who had many references to make on Indian birds.

Baker, E.C. Stuart: *The Indian Ducks and their Allies,* 1908.

*Indian Pigeons and Doves,* 1913.

*The Gamebirds of India, Burma and Ceylon,* 3 vols., 1921.

*The Nidification of Birds of the Indian Empire,* 4 vols., 1932-35.

Bates, R.S.P.: *Bird life in India,* 1931. Good reading.

Beebe, W.: *A Monograph of the Pheasants,* 4 vols., 1918-22. A commendable study.

*Pheasants, their lives and homes,* 2nd ed. 1936, 2 vols. in one. Precursor to his monograph.

Blatter, E. & W.S. Millard: *Some beautiful Indian Trees,* Bombay.

Blyth, E.: *Catalogue of Birds in the Museum of the Asiatic Society,* 1849. Useful reference, specially for historians and taxonomists.

Bor, N.L. & M.B. Raizada: *Some beautiful Indian Climbers and Shrubs.*

Brandis, D.: *Indian Trees.*

Champion, F.W.: *The Jungle in sunlight and shadow.* One of the many publications on wildlife and sport to come out from about 1890 to 1930.

Delacour, J.: *The Pheasants of the World.*

Dewar, D.: *Glimpses of Indian Birds,* 1913. By the author of several guides on Indian bird-life.

Fletcher, T.B. & C.M. Inglis: *Birds of an Indian Garden,* 1964.

Freeman Michael: *The Complete Book of Wildlife & Nature Photography,* Simon & Schuster, New York, 1981.

Gee, E.P.: *The Wild Life of India,* 1924

Gould, J.A.: *A Century of Birds from the Himalaya mountains,* 1832. The first of the author's varied and vast folio. Includes some familiar prints, used also on table mats and other artefacts.

Gray, J.E.: *Illustrations of Indian Zoology,* 2 vols., 1830-35. Includes a detailed atlas and is a valuable historical compendium.

Henderson, G. & A.O. Hume: *Lahore to Yarkand,* 1873. Focuses on the natural history of the regions traversed during the journey. The extensive section on birds was reprinted as an independent monograph by Hume, under the title 'Contribution to Indian Ornithology'.

Henry, G.M.: *Coloured Plates of the Birds of Ceylon,* 1927.

Kingston, R.W.: *A Naturalist in Himalaya,* 1920, Primarily insects.

*A naturalist in Hindustan,* 1923.

# Glossary

**Adult:** a bird that has attained complete developmental growth and the final plumage of its species. Many birds may breed before this stage. Several species undergo seasonal moulting even after adulthood, but their pattern does not change with age.

**Arboreal:** spending most or large part of its time in trees.

**Avian:** of, or pertaining to, birds

**Avifauna:** the total bird diversity of an area.

**Biogeography:** (biology + geography); division and study of various regions from the point of view of distribution of wildlife.

**Community:** set of populations that interact with one another in a specific area.

**Crepuscular:** active during the twilight hours, both morning and evening.

**Dimorphism:** existing in two forms (of plumage) or phases.

**Diurnal:** active by day.

**Ecosystem:** dynamic, interacting complex of life forms and environmental factors in an area, taken as a self-sufficient unit.

**Family:** taxonomic unit, used to denote a group of closely related animals or birds; a collection of related genera.

**Feathers:** the largest plumes on a bird's body.

**Fledging:** a stage in feather growth when the chick is (usually) able to leave nest.

**Gregarious:** by habit, given to congregating or gathering in large numbers.

**Hawking:** capturing insect prey in flight (usually with bill, but also with feet).

**Immature:** individual that has grown to its full size, but has not yet attained adult plumage.

**Incubation:** aiding embryonic development in the egg by warming it; birds may do this by sitting on the eggs, or by placing them in spots where warmth is available e.g. compost.

**Jheel:** Indian term for wetland or lake, usually with submerged as well as emergent vegetation.

**Migration:** cyclic, seasonal journeys made between breeding and wintering quarters.

**Nest Parasitism:** phenomenon in which parent bird builds no nest, but dupes another bird into incubating its egg and rearing the young, by placing its own egg among the latter's. Widespread in the cuckoo family.

**Nocturnal:** active by night.

**Nuptial:** connected with courtship and mating.

**Polyandry:** (of female) having more than one mate (male) at the same time.

**Polygamy:** (of male) having more than one mate (female) at the same time.

**Polymorphism:** occurrence in more than two forms (plumage).

**Plumage:** collective term for the total complement of colours, feathers, adornments and other structural appendages of a bird.

**Precocial:** chicks which are feathered and active on hatching (as opposed to altricial chicks, which are naked and helpless at birth).

**Spatulate:** (of bill) shaped like a spoon or spatula.

**Tank:** large (artificial) lake or reservoir; usually applied to waterworks or irrigation structures.

**Terrestrial:** spending most or large part of its time on land.

**Wildlife:** all the uncultivated/ undomesticated flora and fauna of an area.

# Index

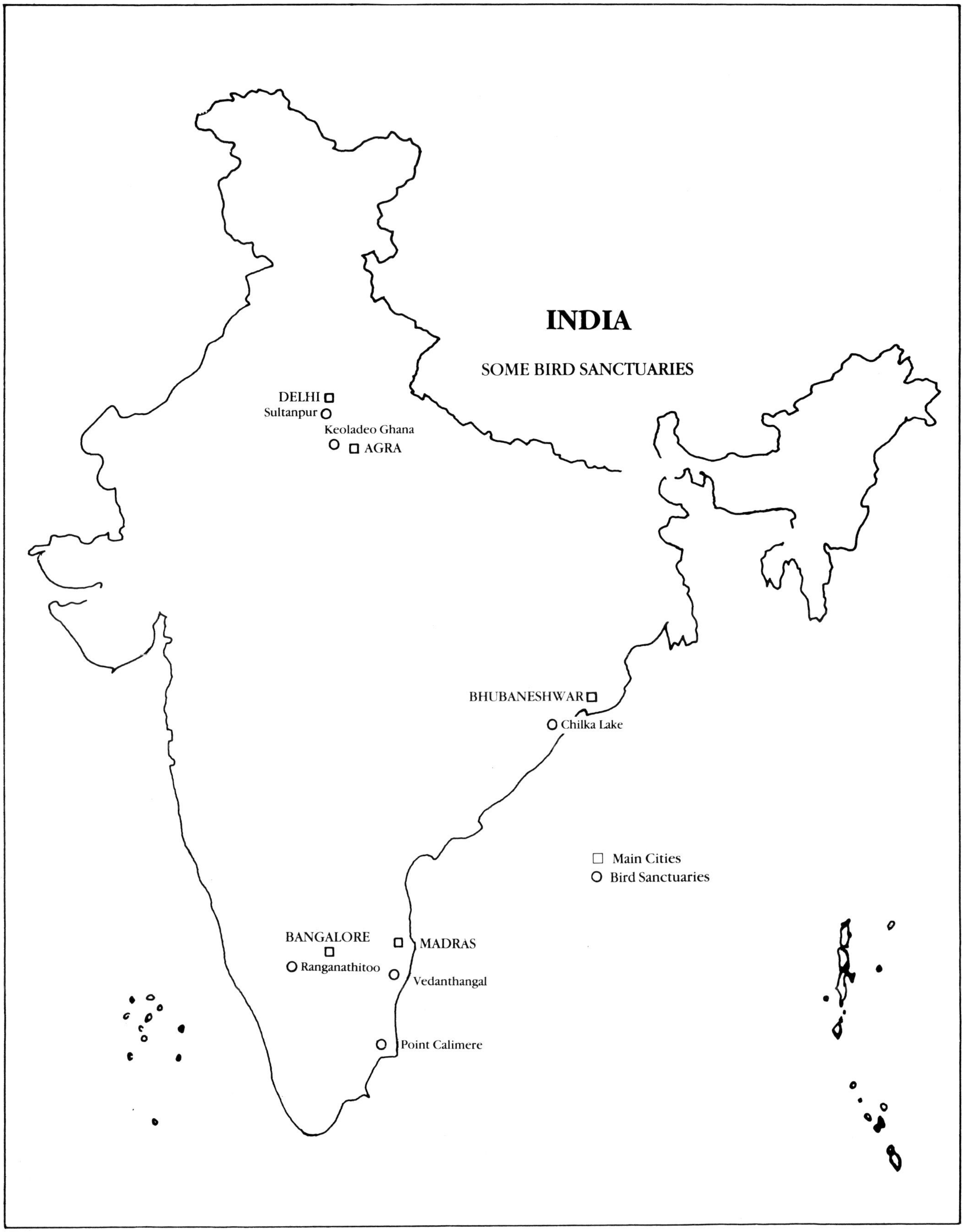
INDIA
SOME BIRD SANCTUARIES
DELHI
Sultanpur
Keoladeo Ghana
AGRA
BHUBANESHWAR
Chilka Lake
Main Cities
Bird Sanctuaries
BANGALORE
MADRAS
Ranganathitoo
Vedanthangal
Point Calimere

## PHOTOGRAPHERS CREDITS

Rajesh Bedi: p.52-53 Great crested grebe
p.67 Crested serpent eagle

Sharad Gaur: p. 57 Comb duck
p. 65 Brahminy kite
p. 82 Oystercatcher
p. 85 Avocet
p. 94 House Swift
p. 96 Blue jay (anting)
p.104 Mynas jousting